Vintage Coloring Book

Flowers and Floral Designs

66 Vintage Floral and Botanical Stress
Relief Coloring Pages for Adults and Grown-Ups

Mia Blackwood

www.southshorepublications.com

Copyright © 2015 SouthShore Publications

ISBN-13: 978-1519546098

ISBN-10: 1519546092

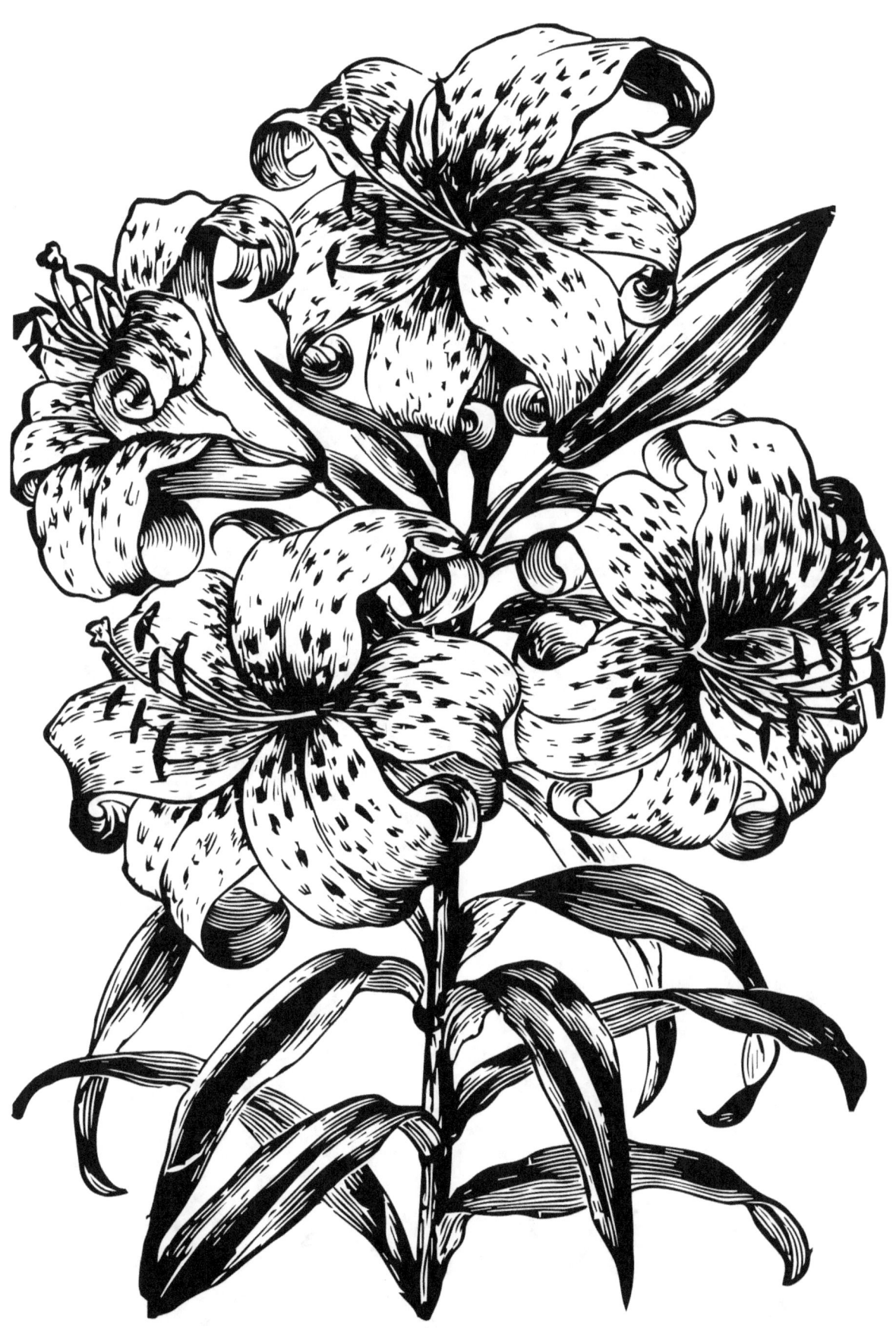

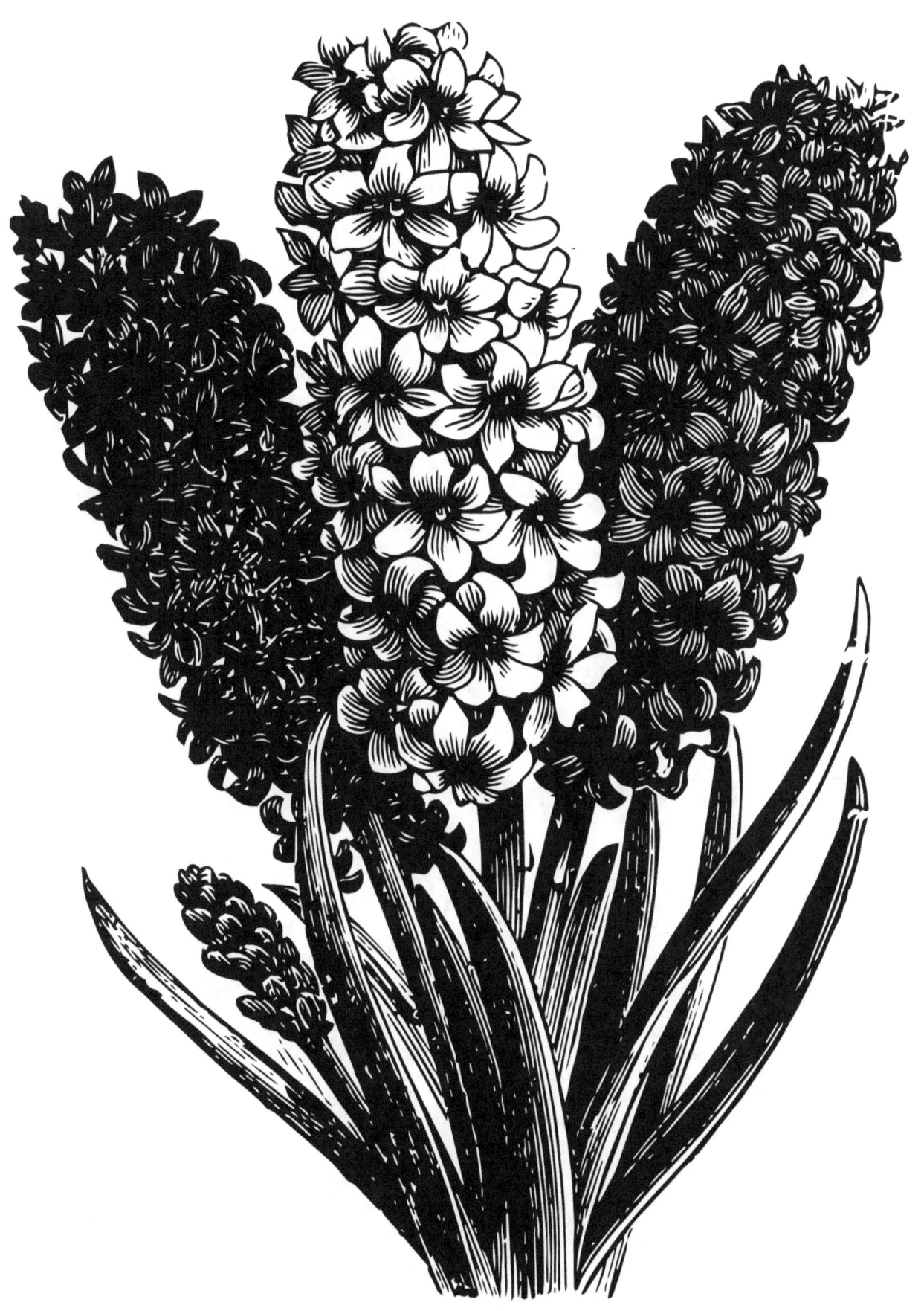

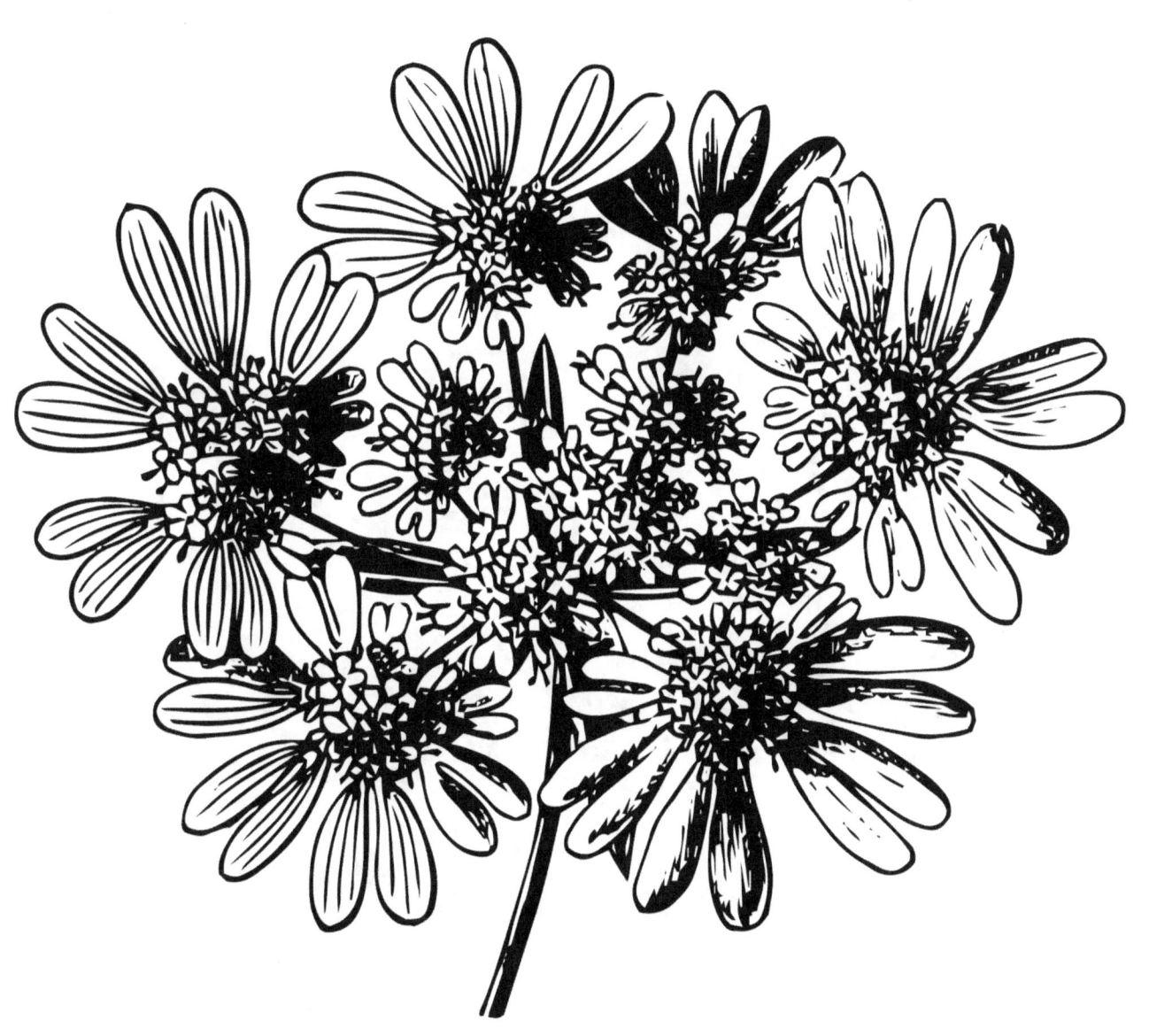

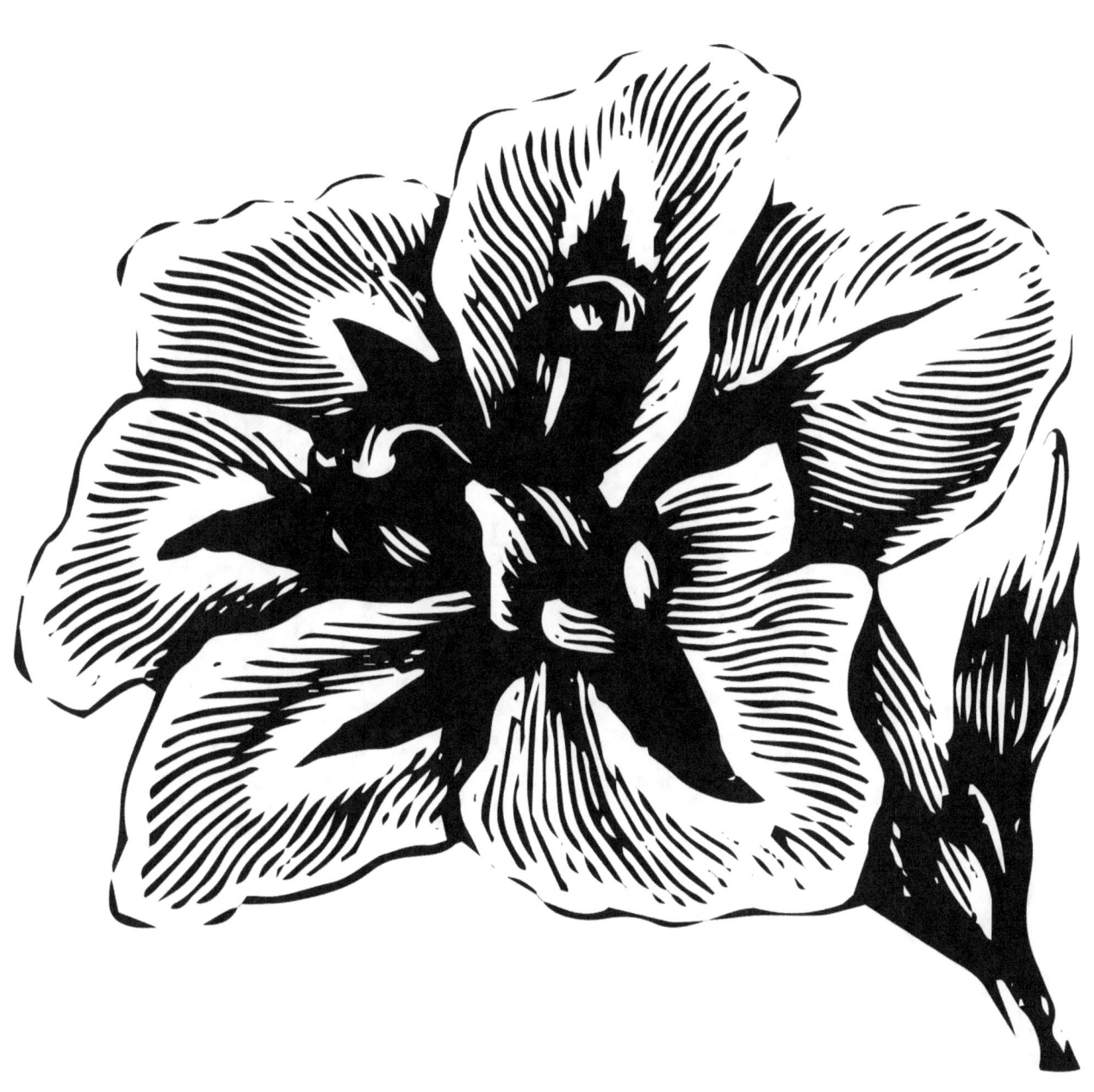

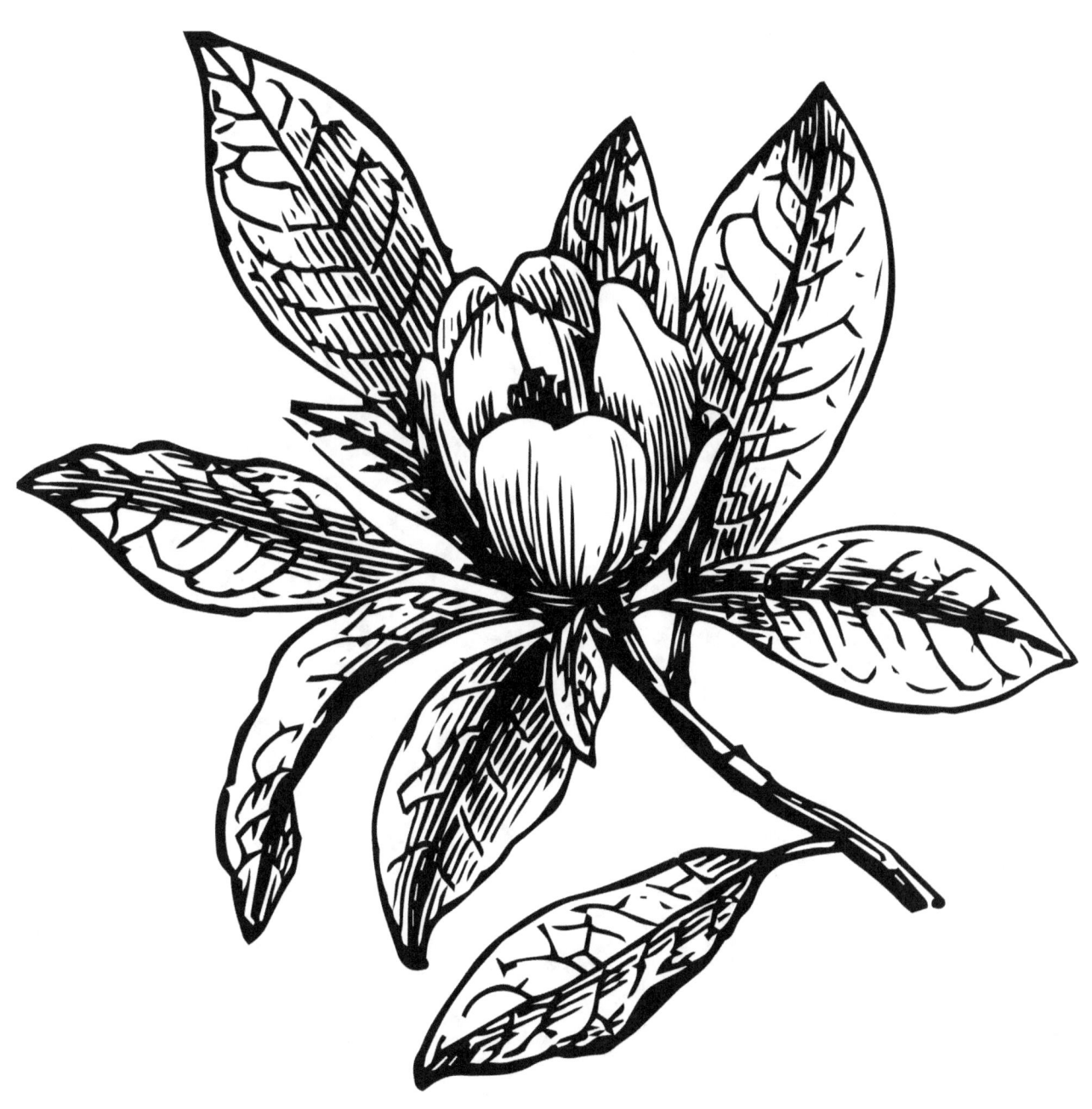

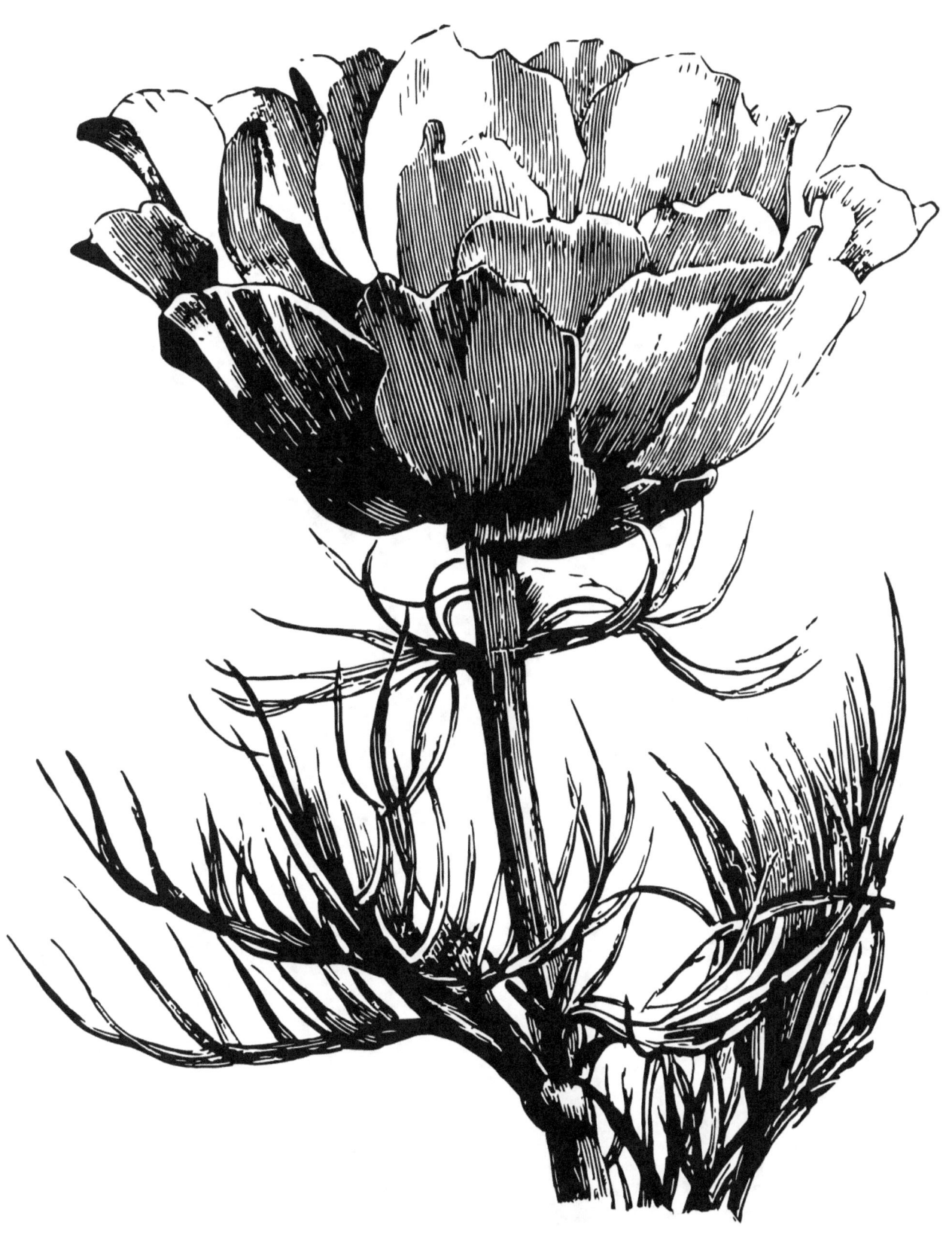

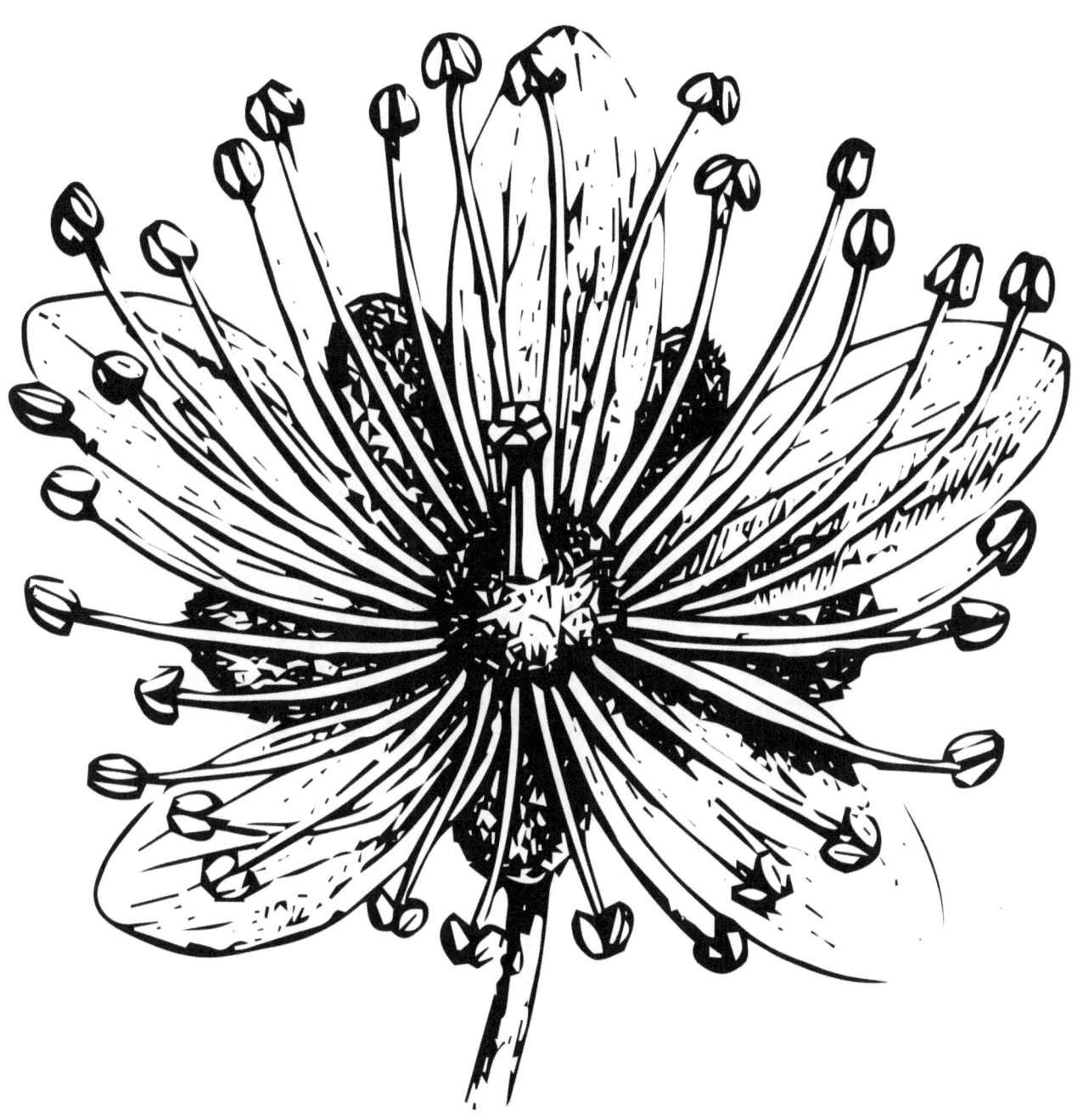

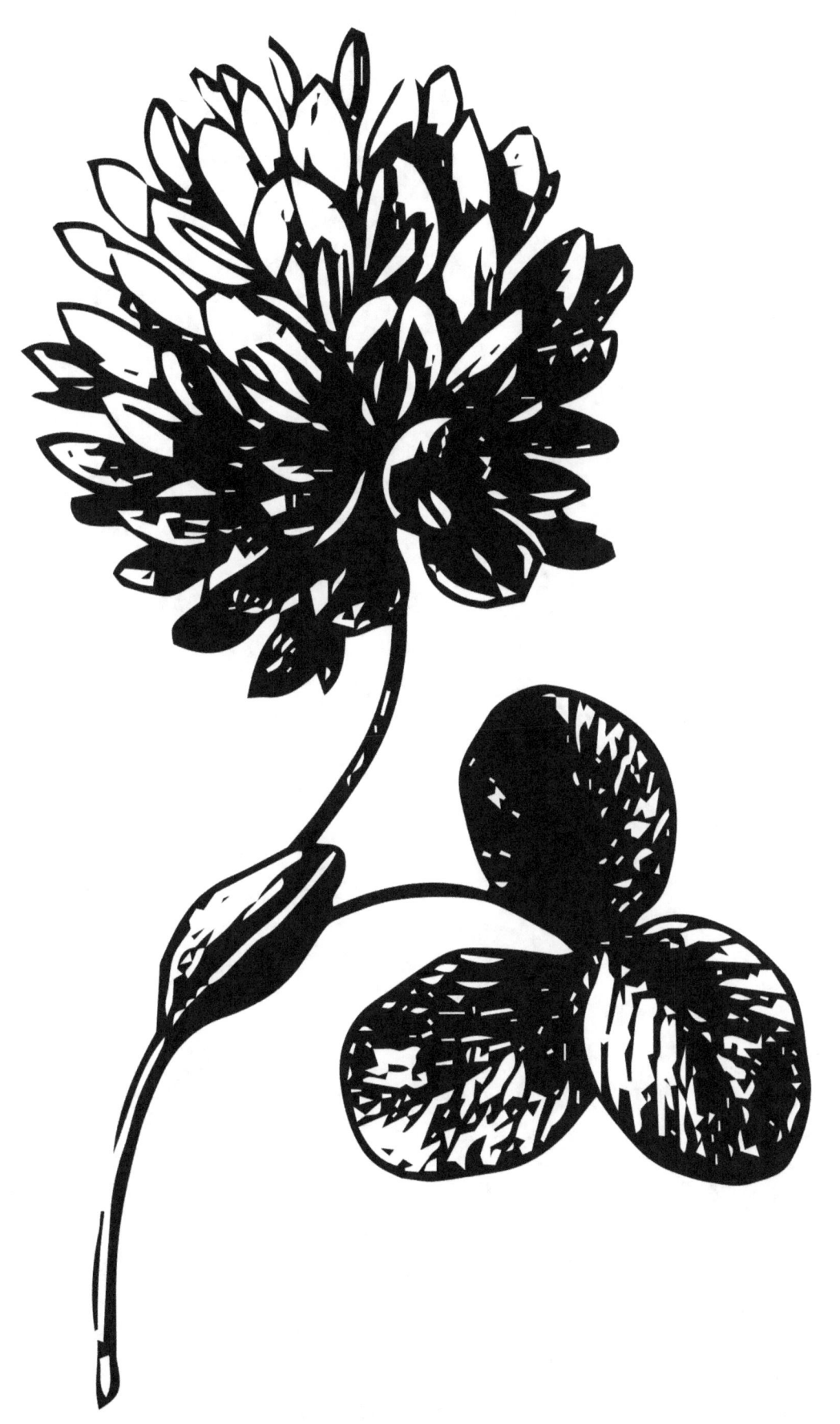

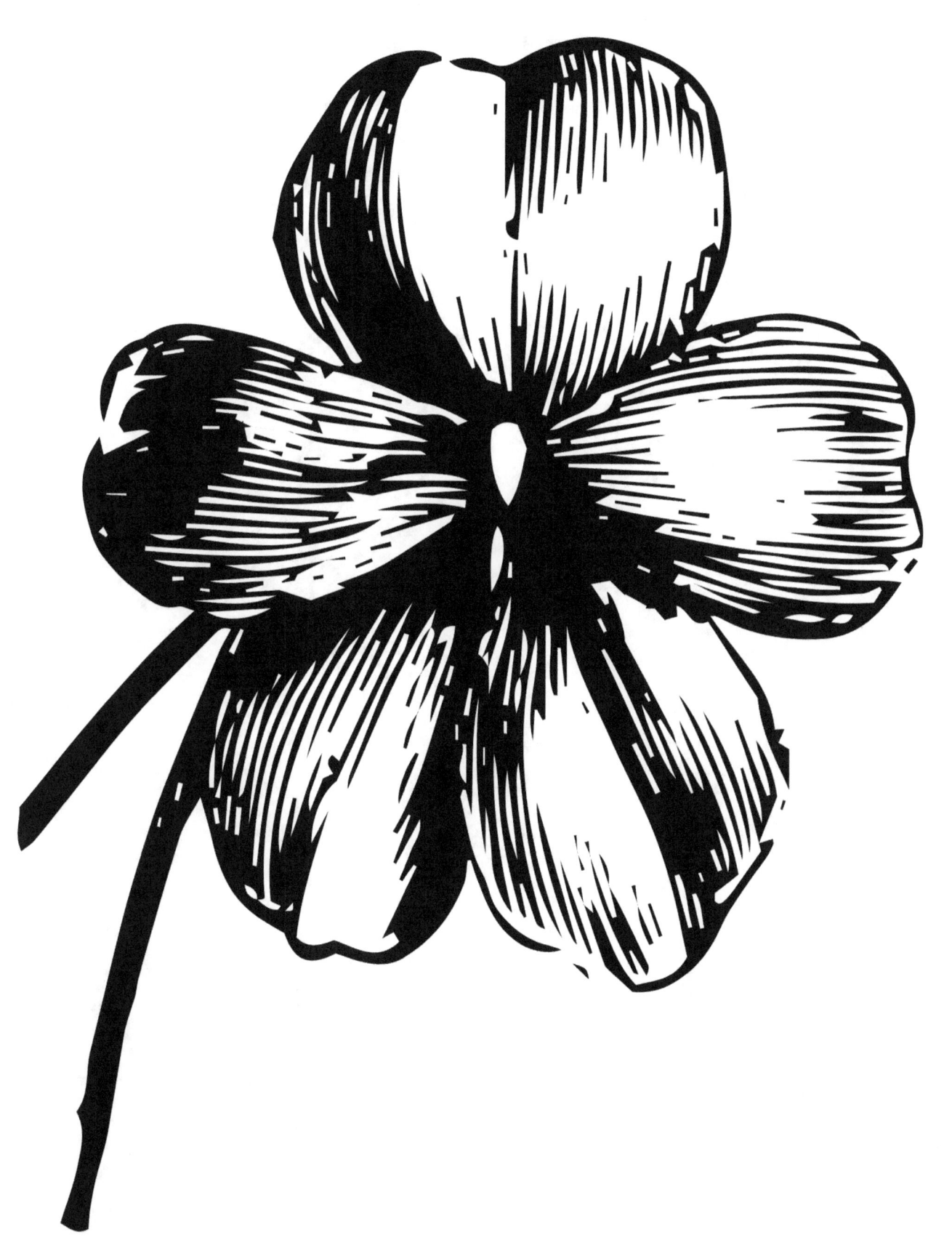

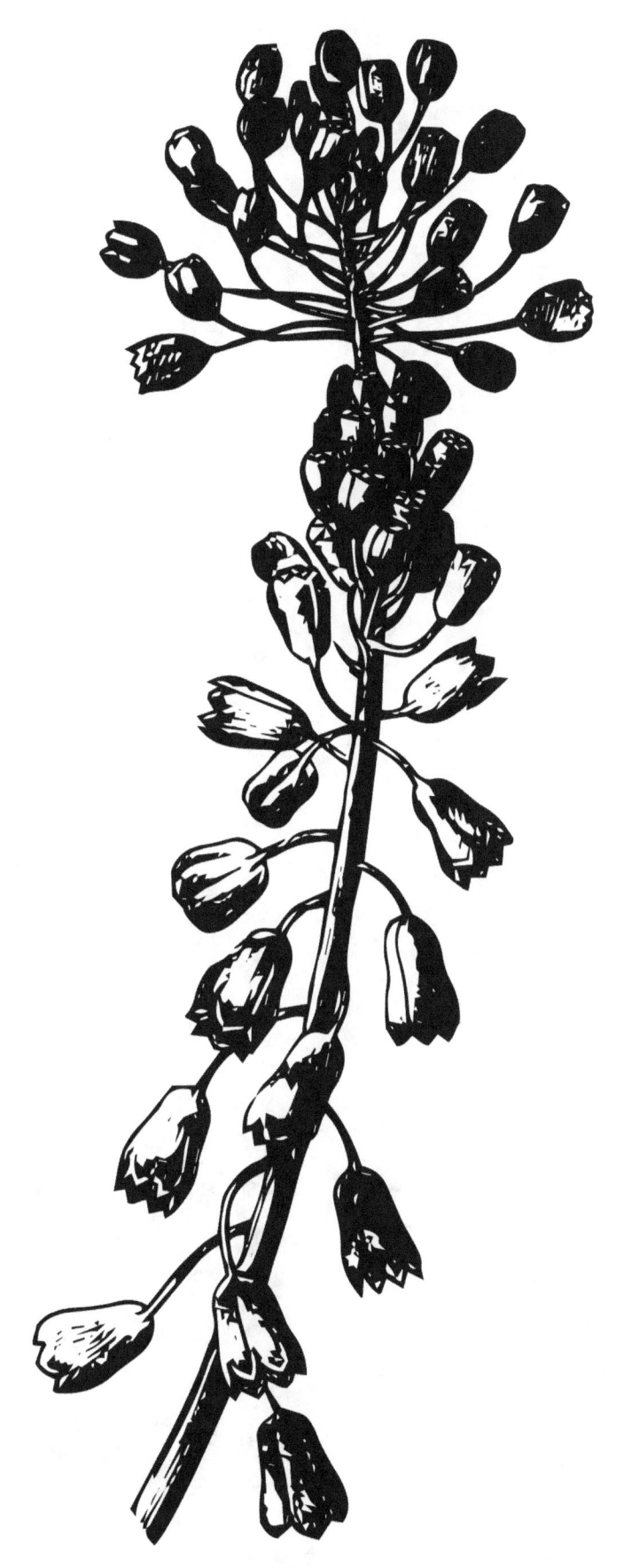

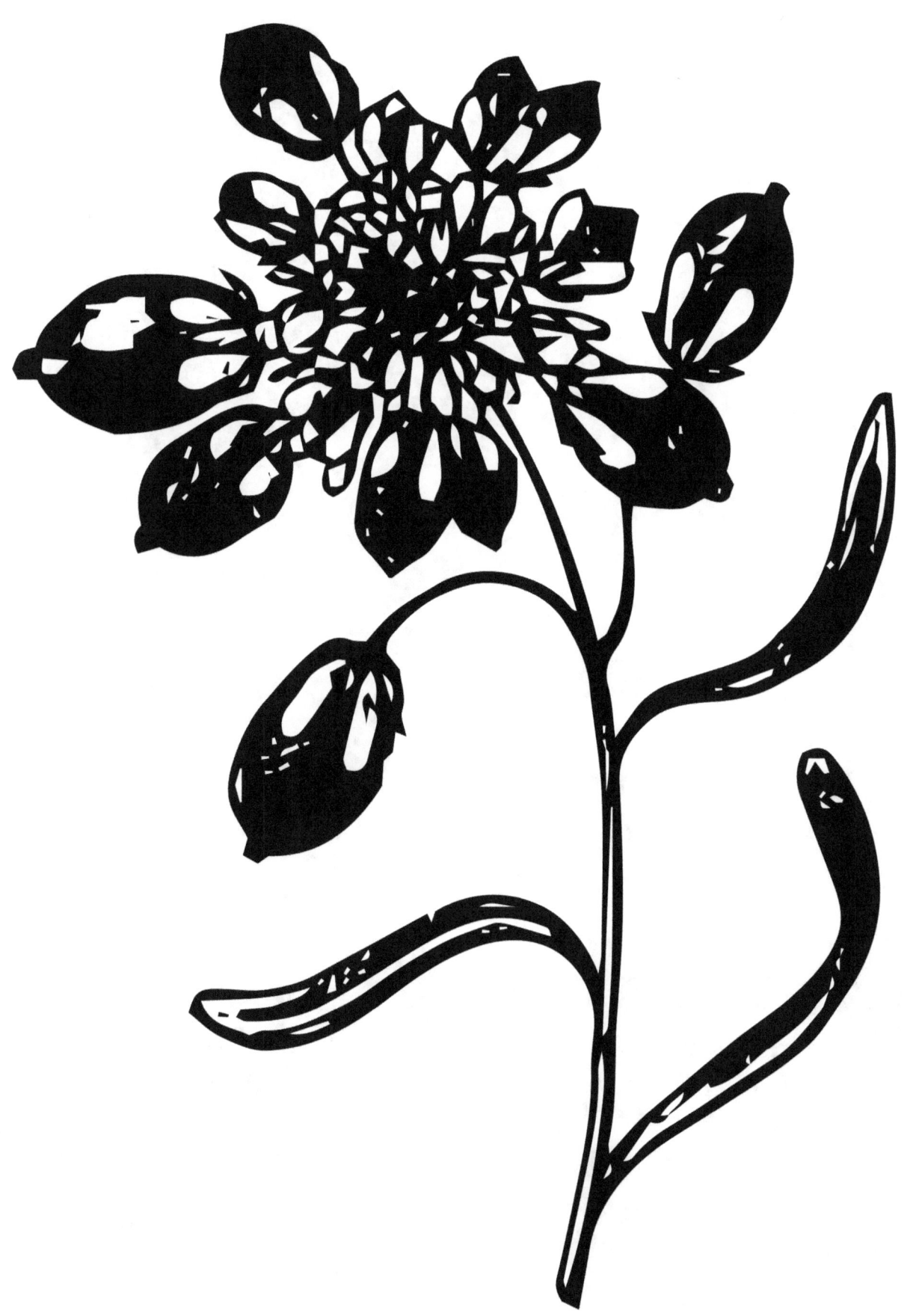

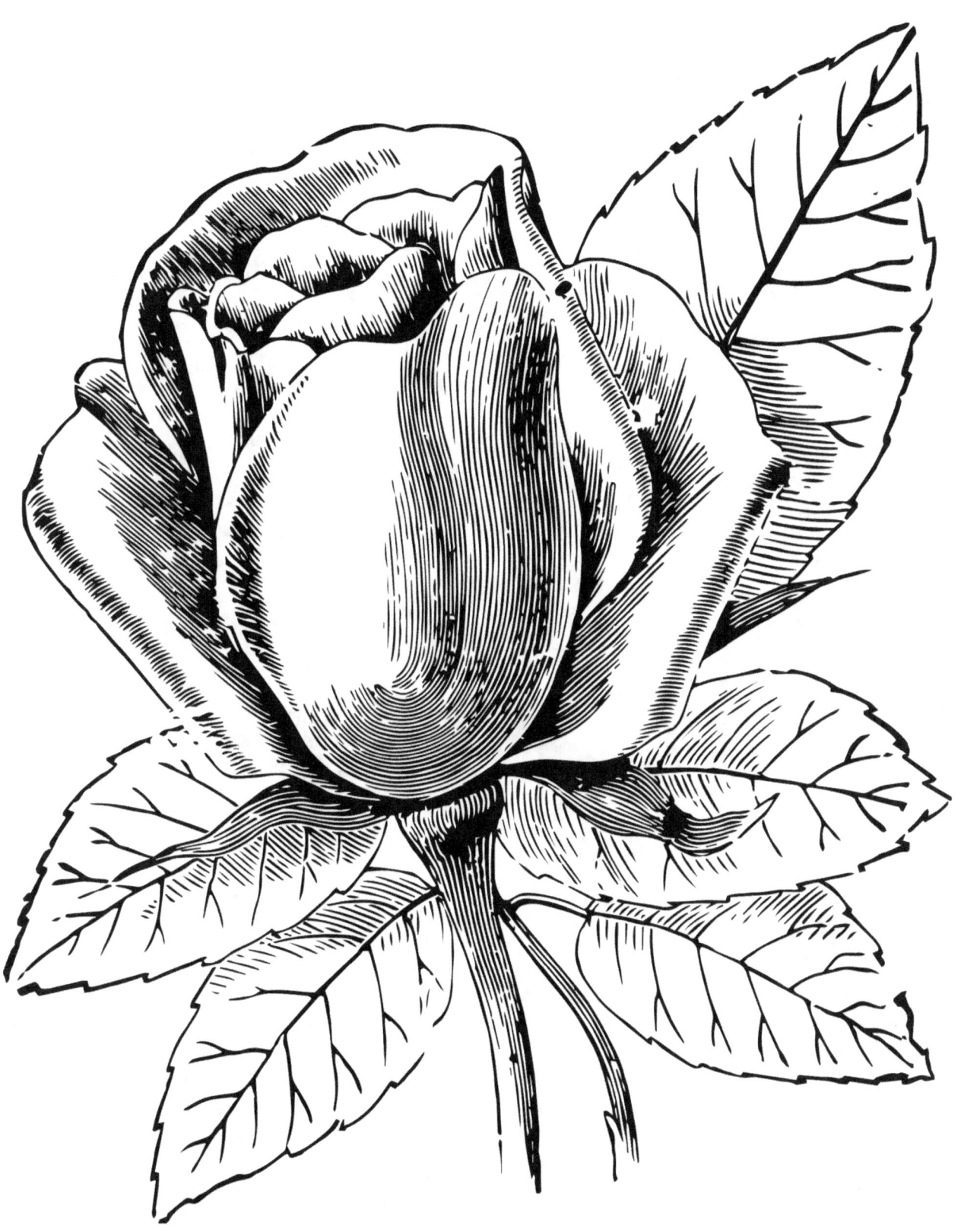

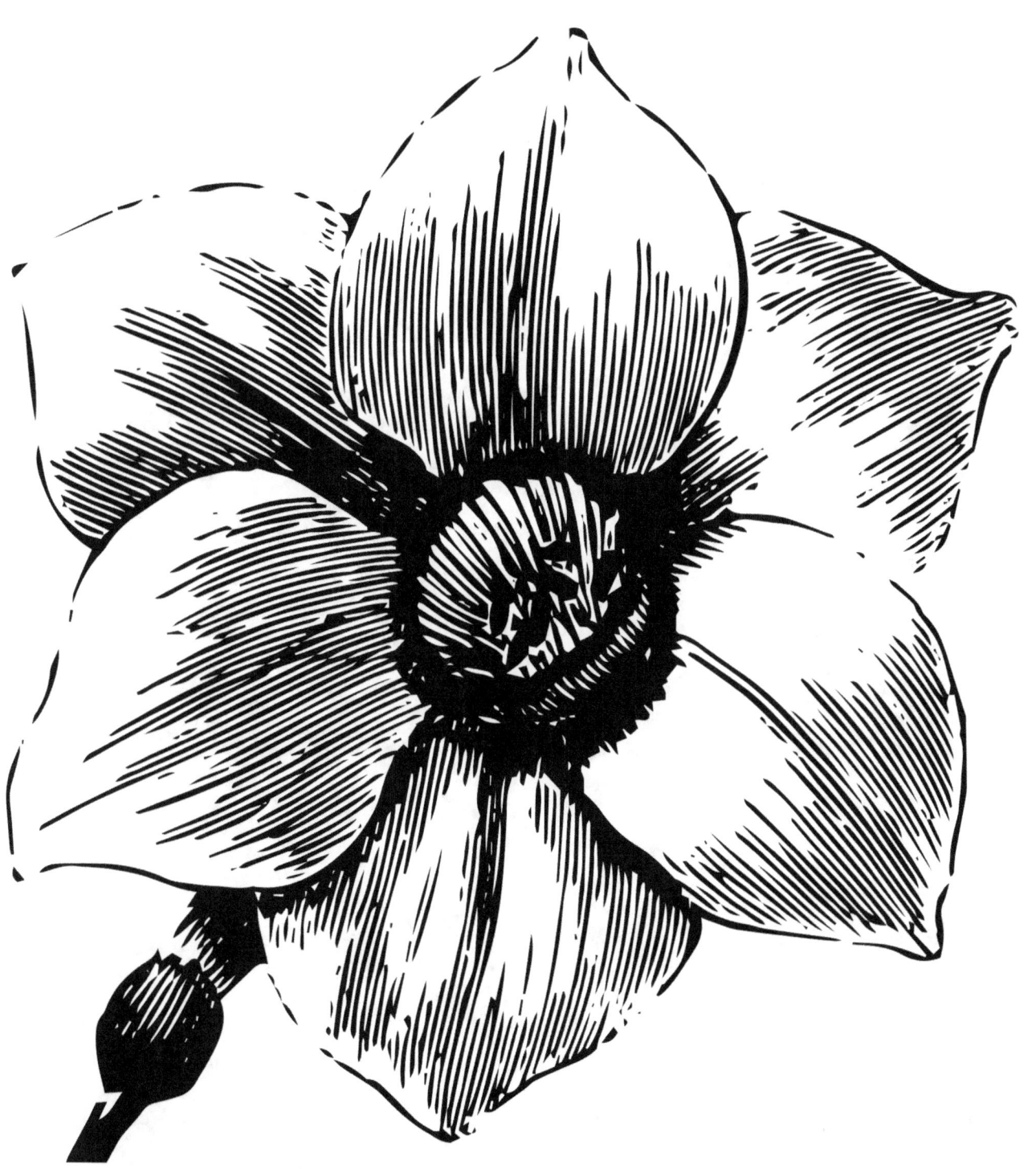

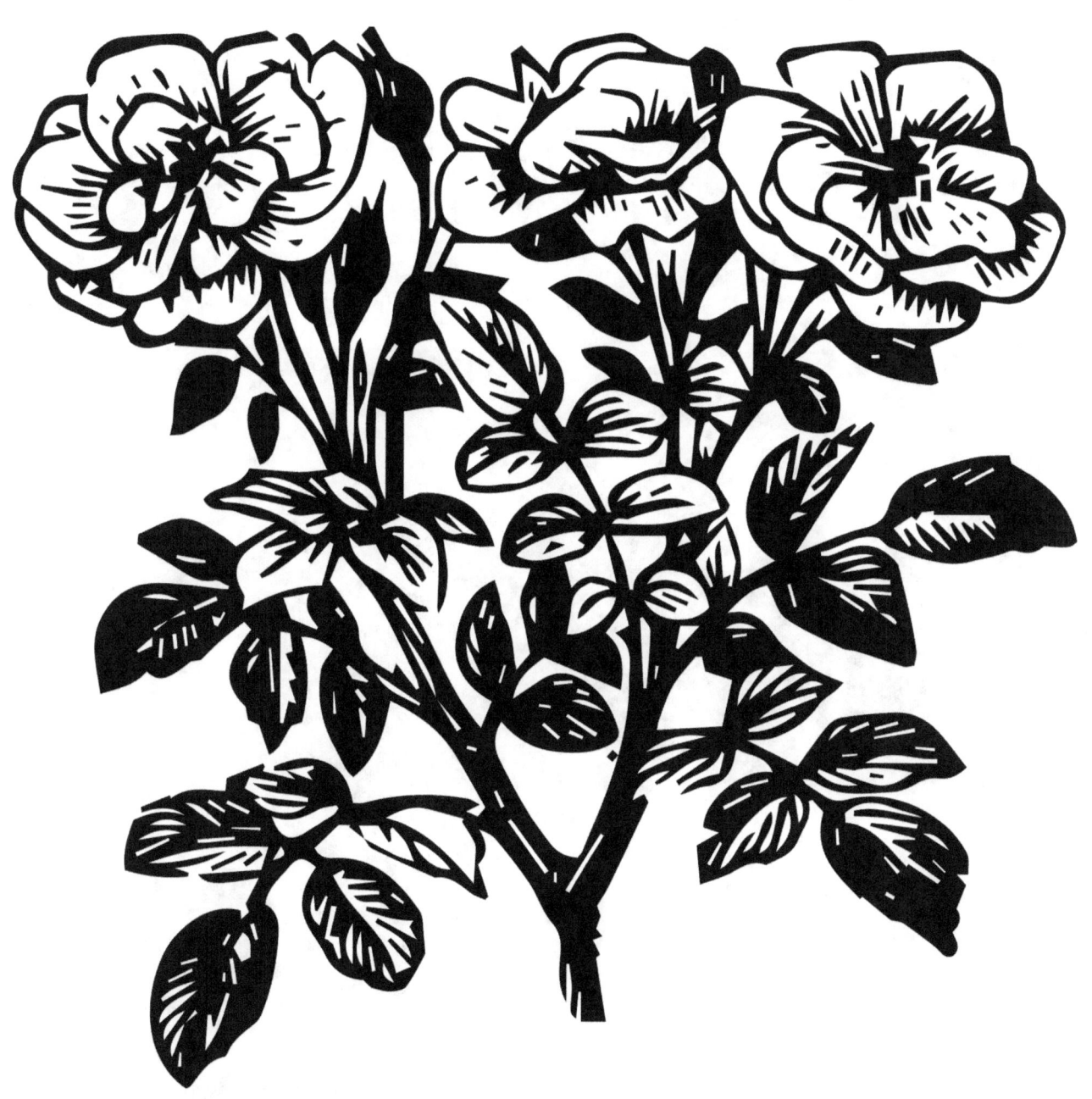

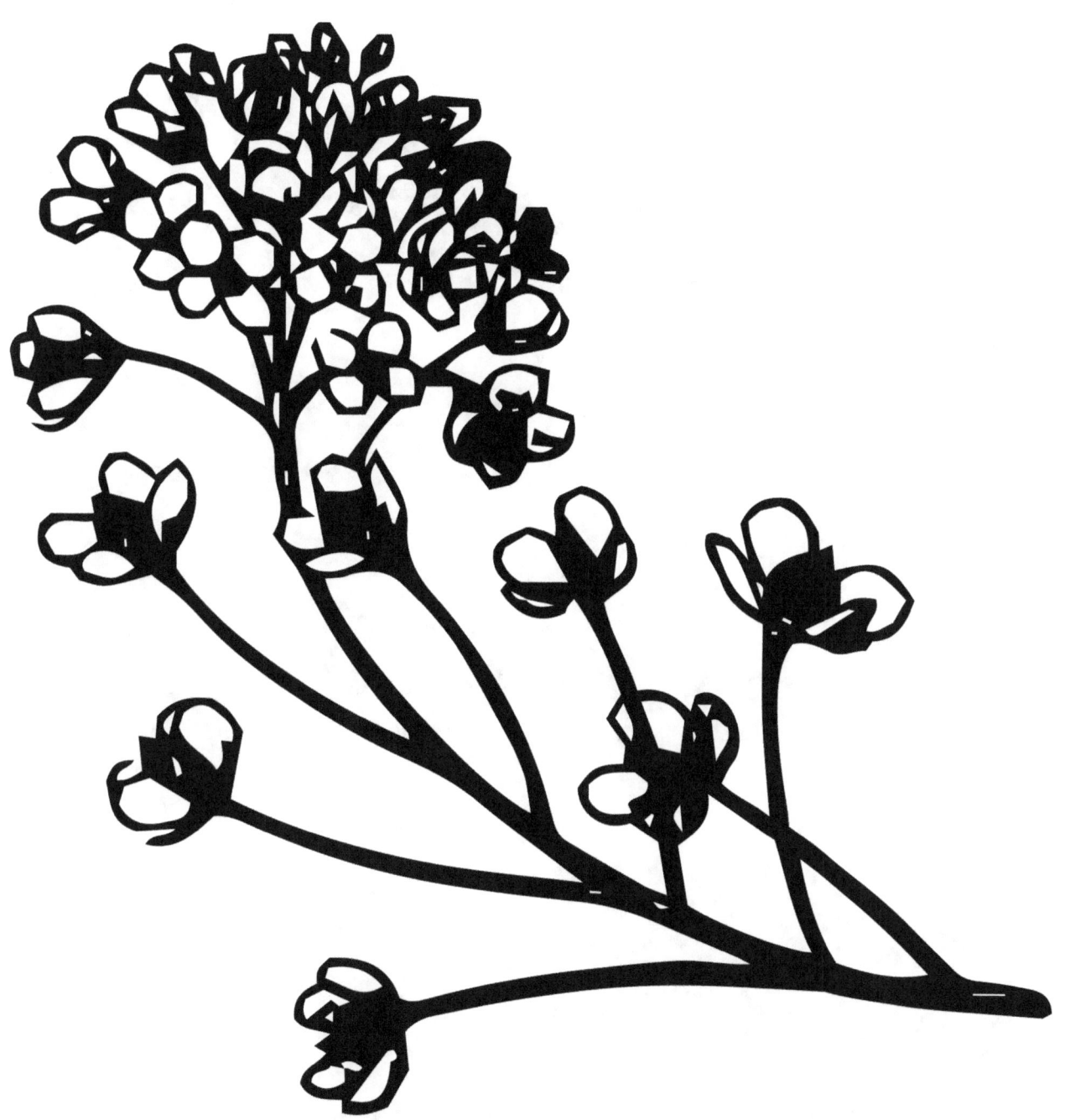

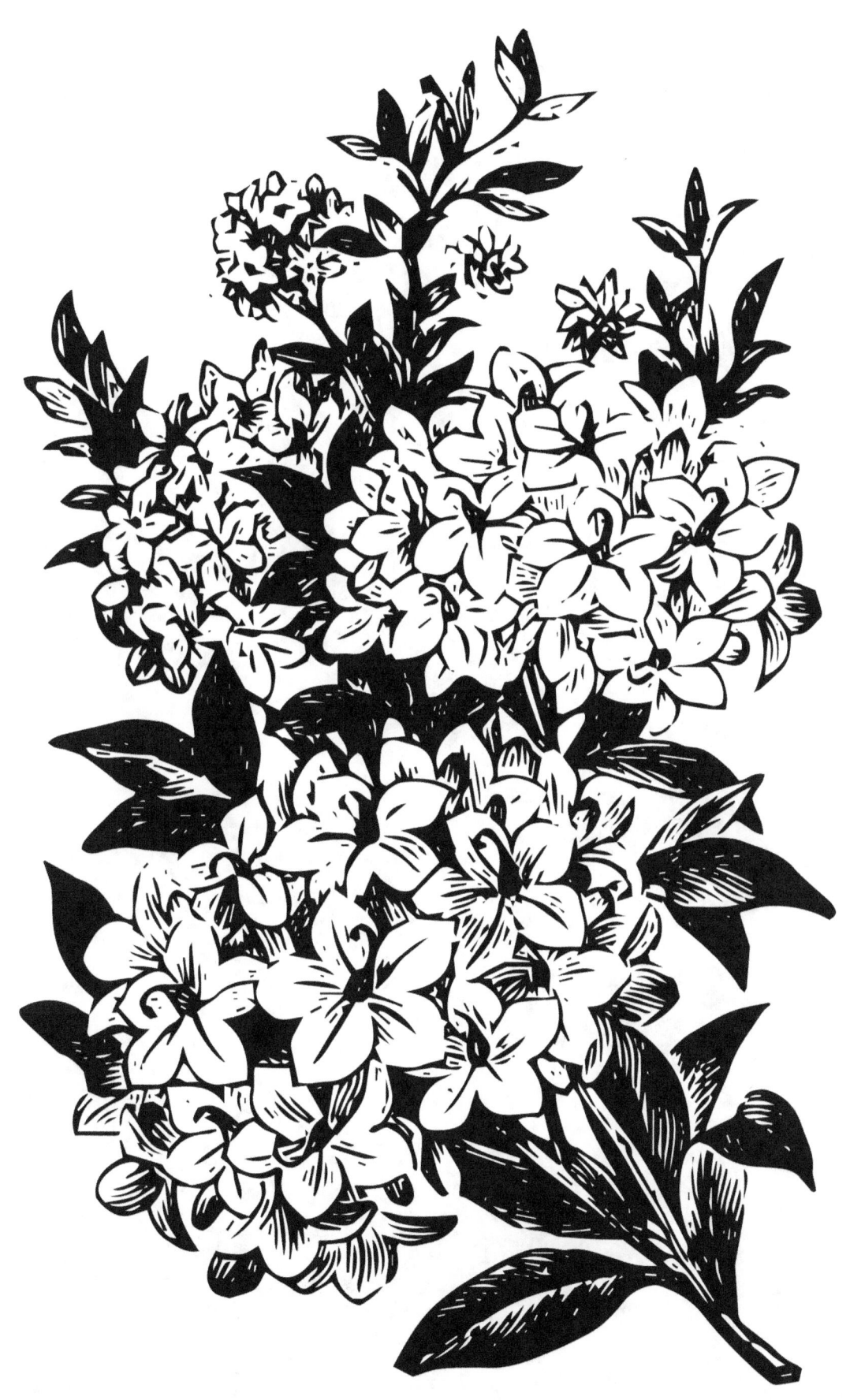

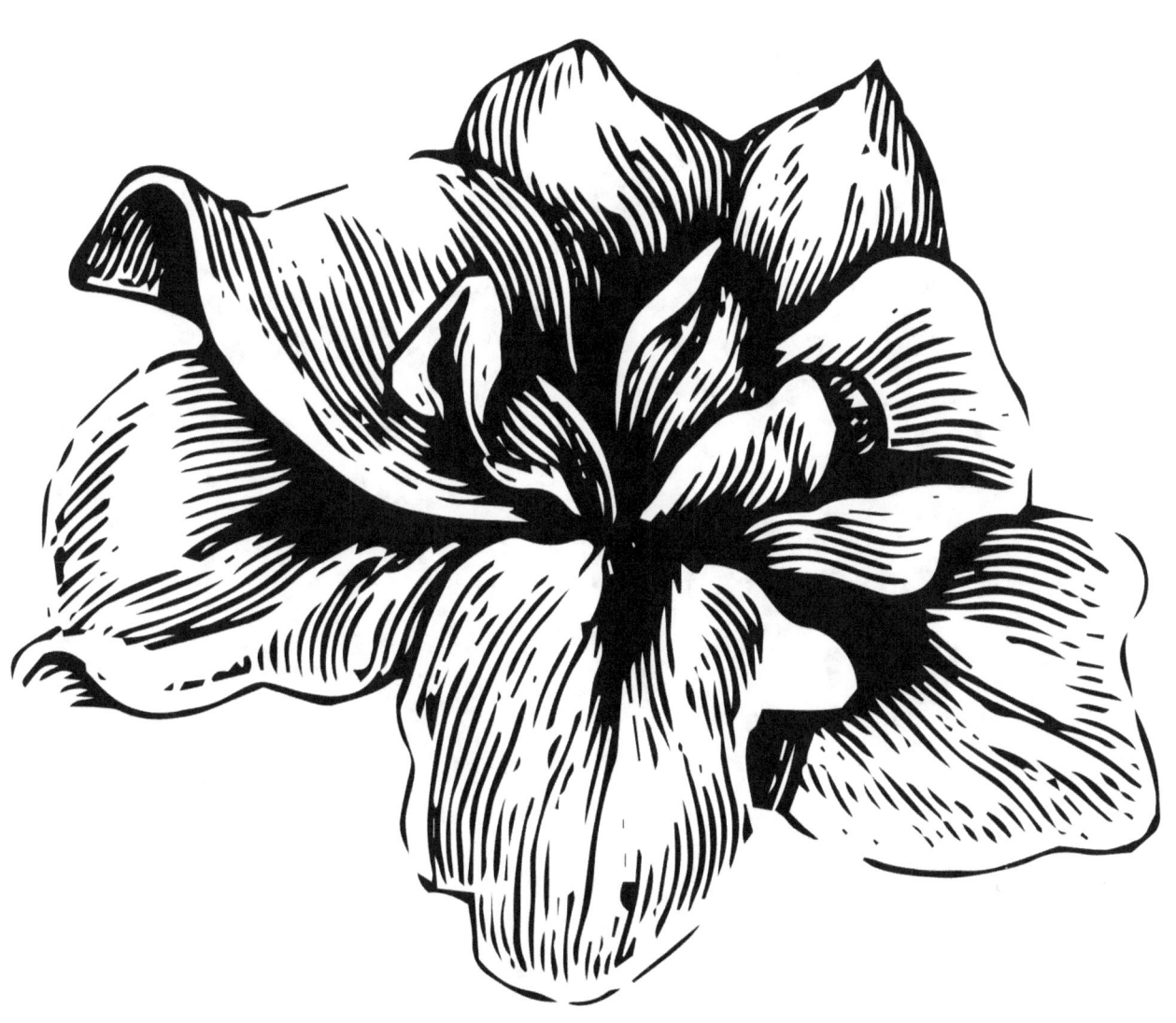

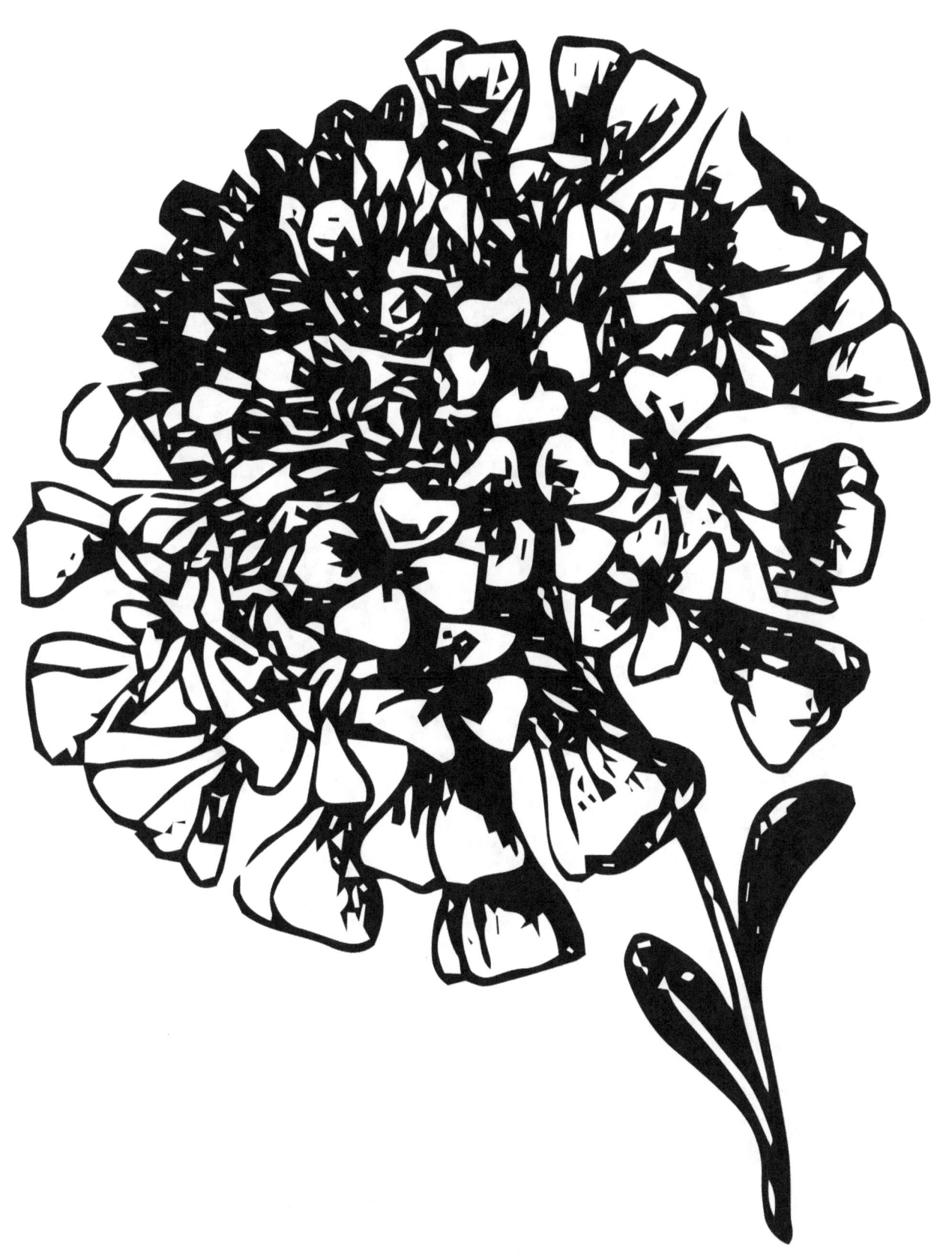

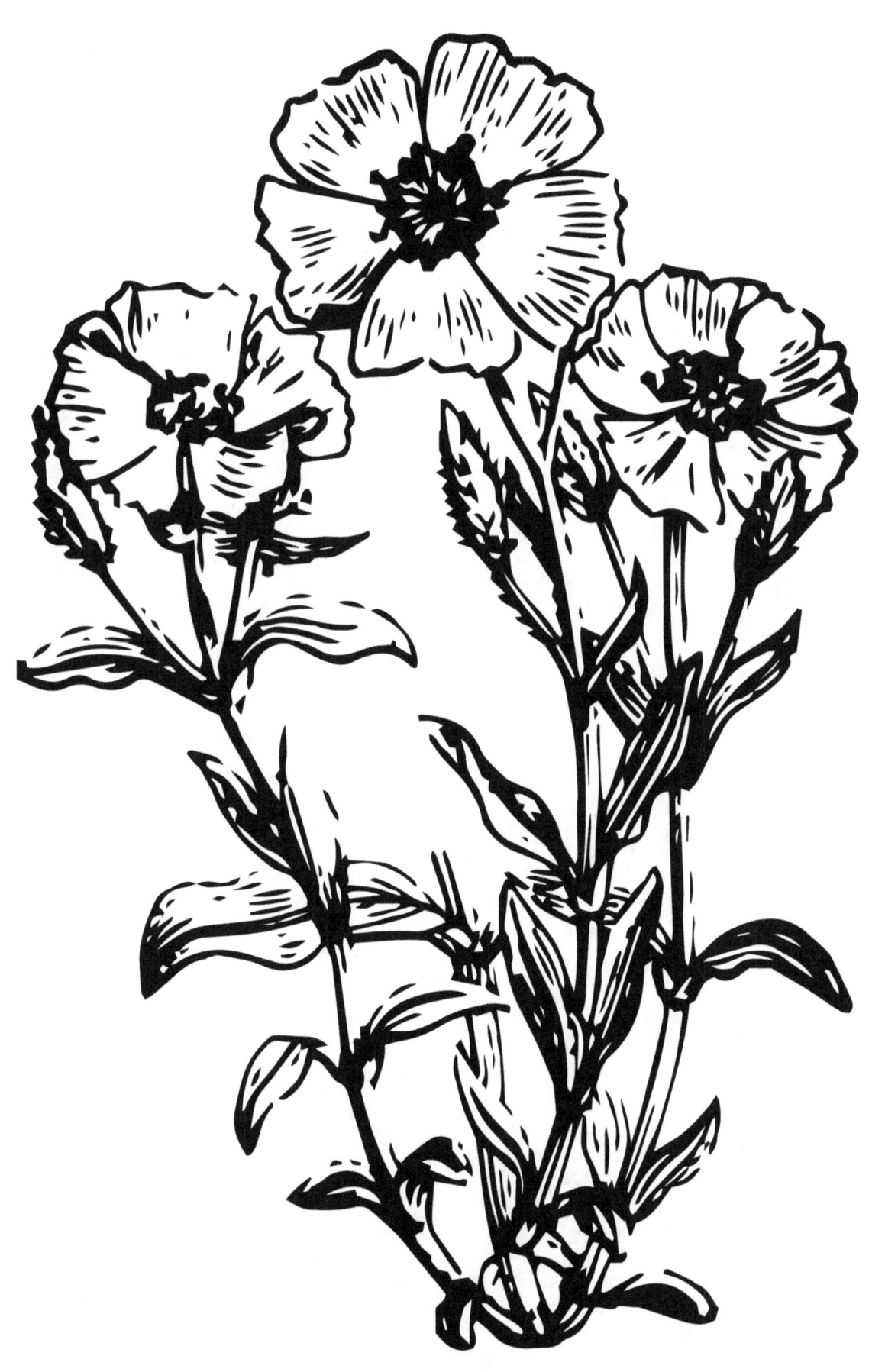

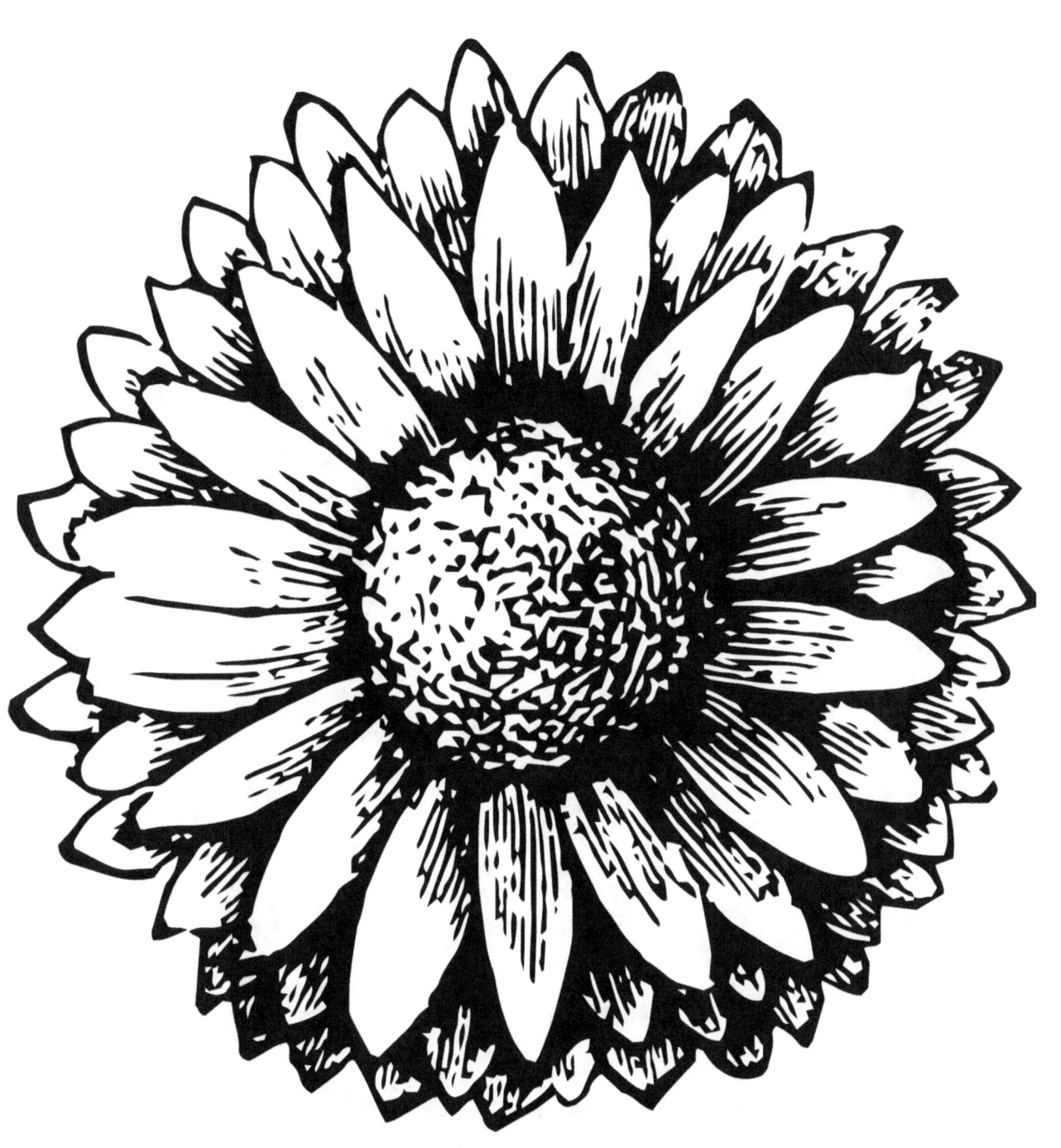

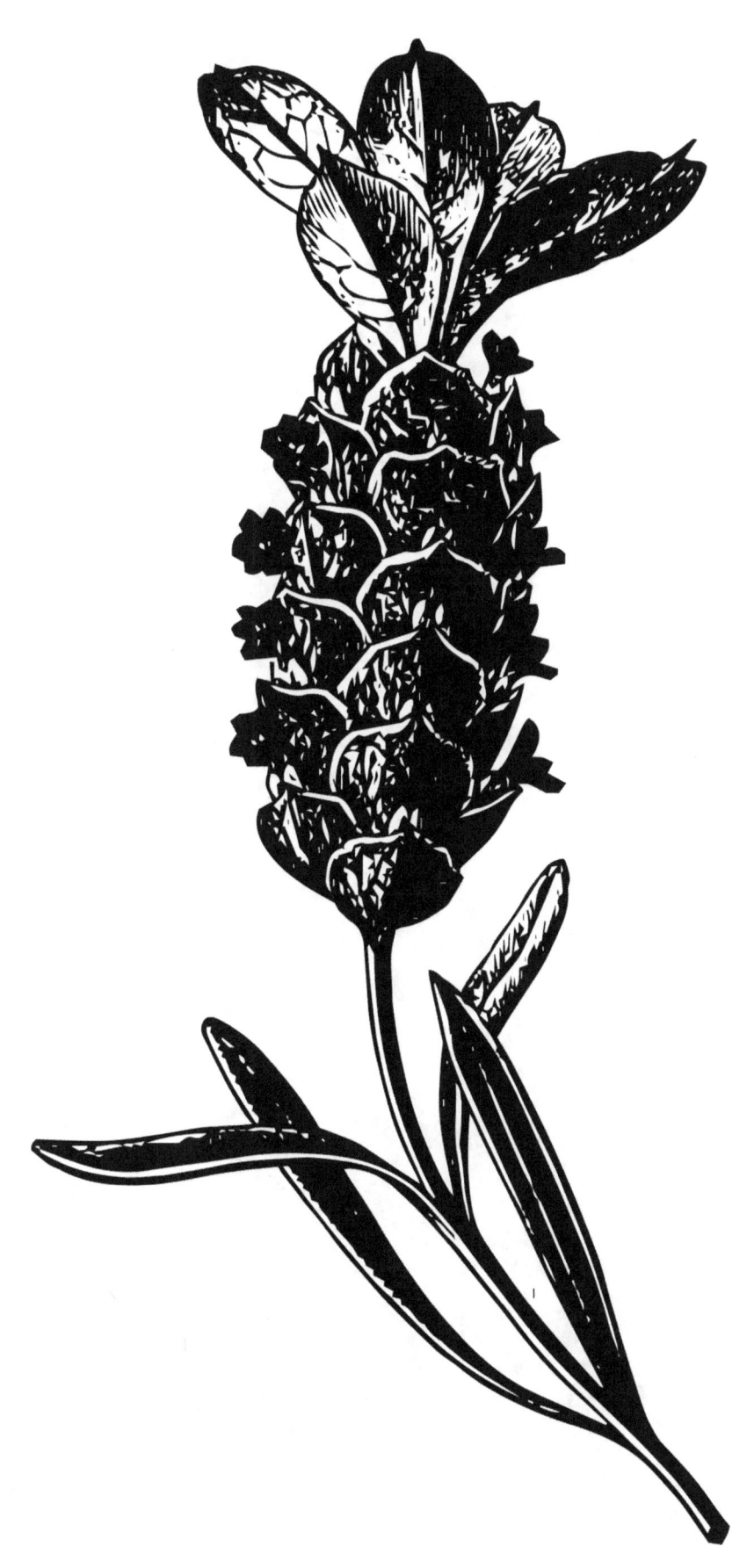

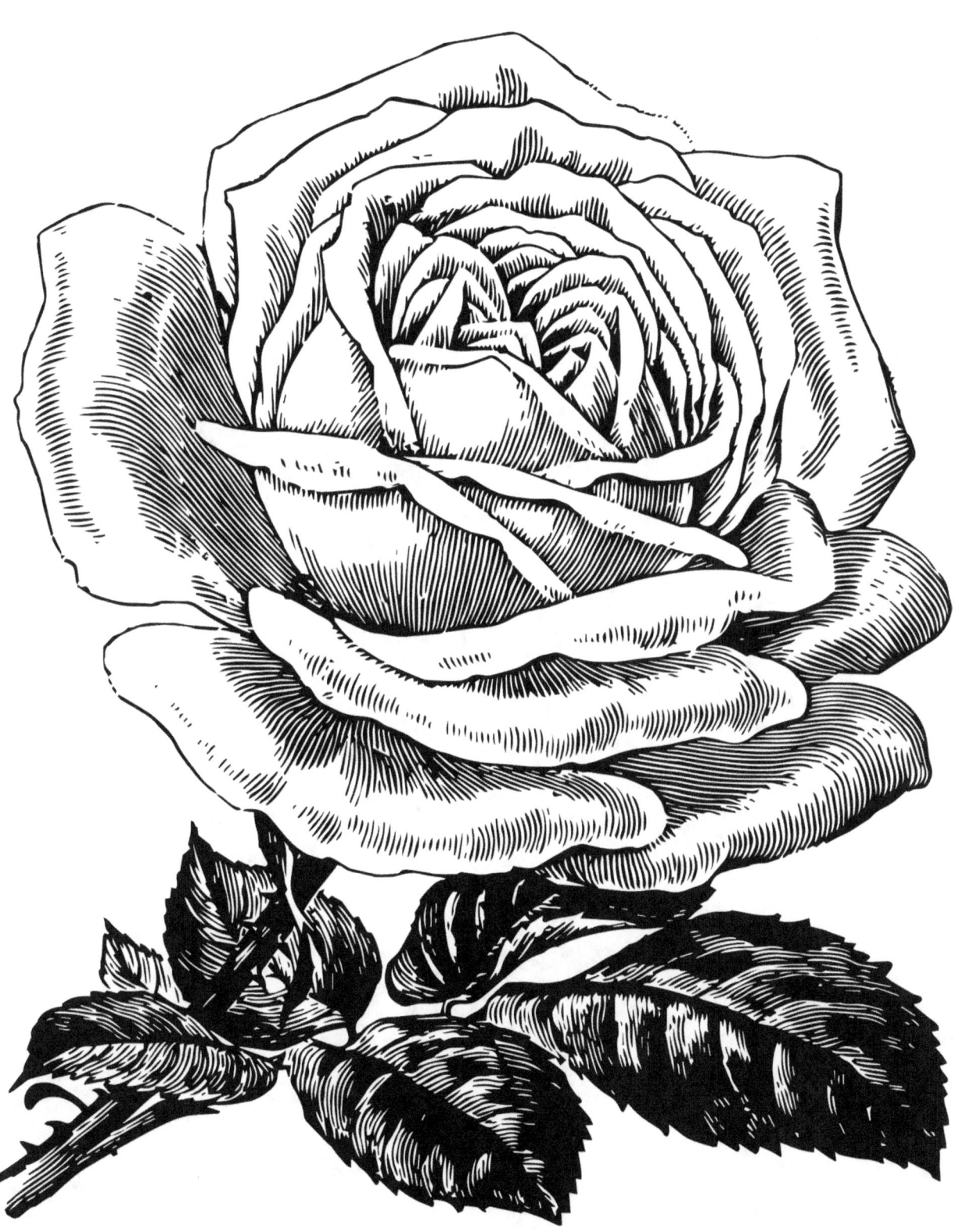

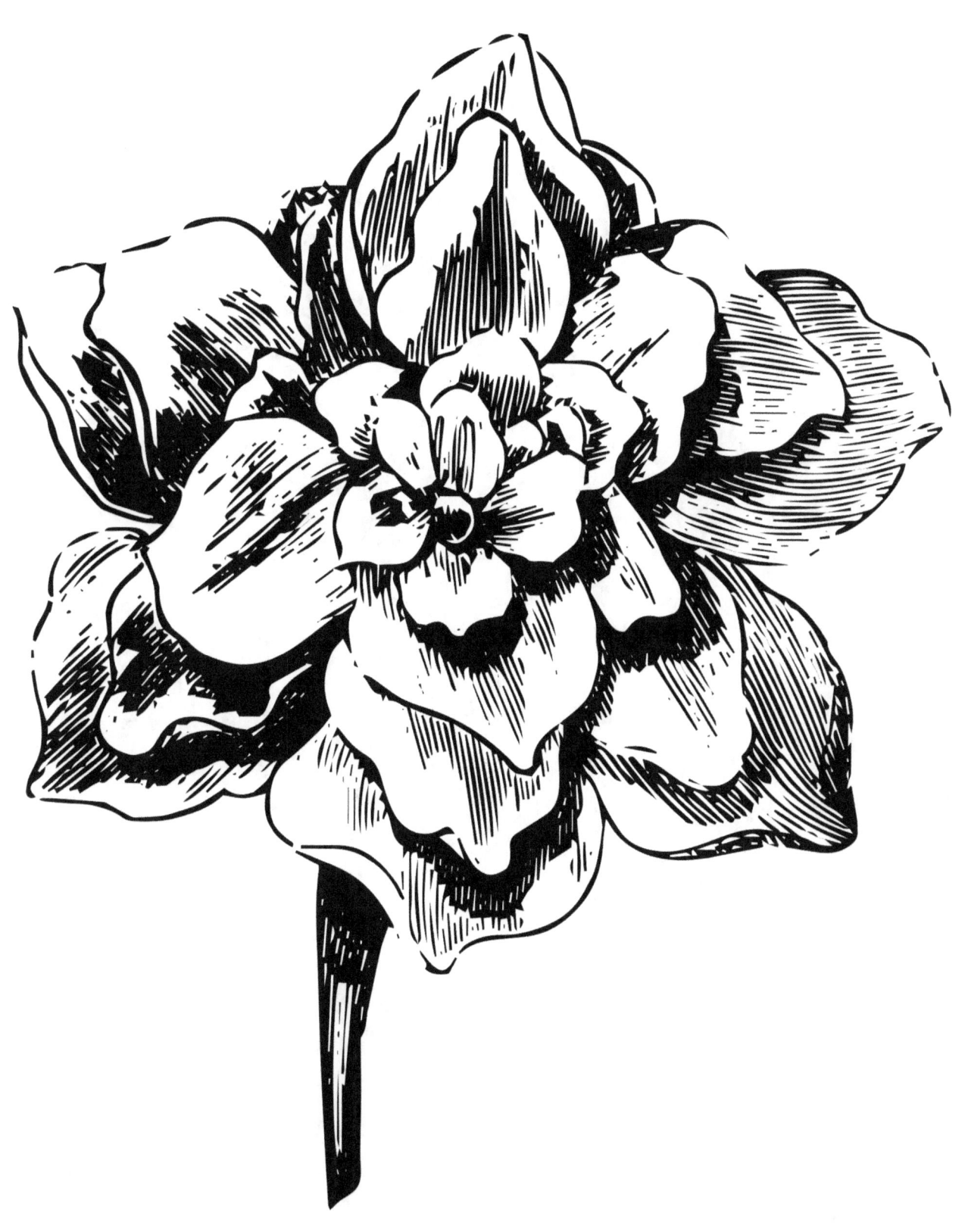

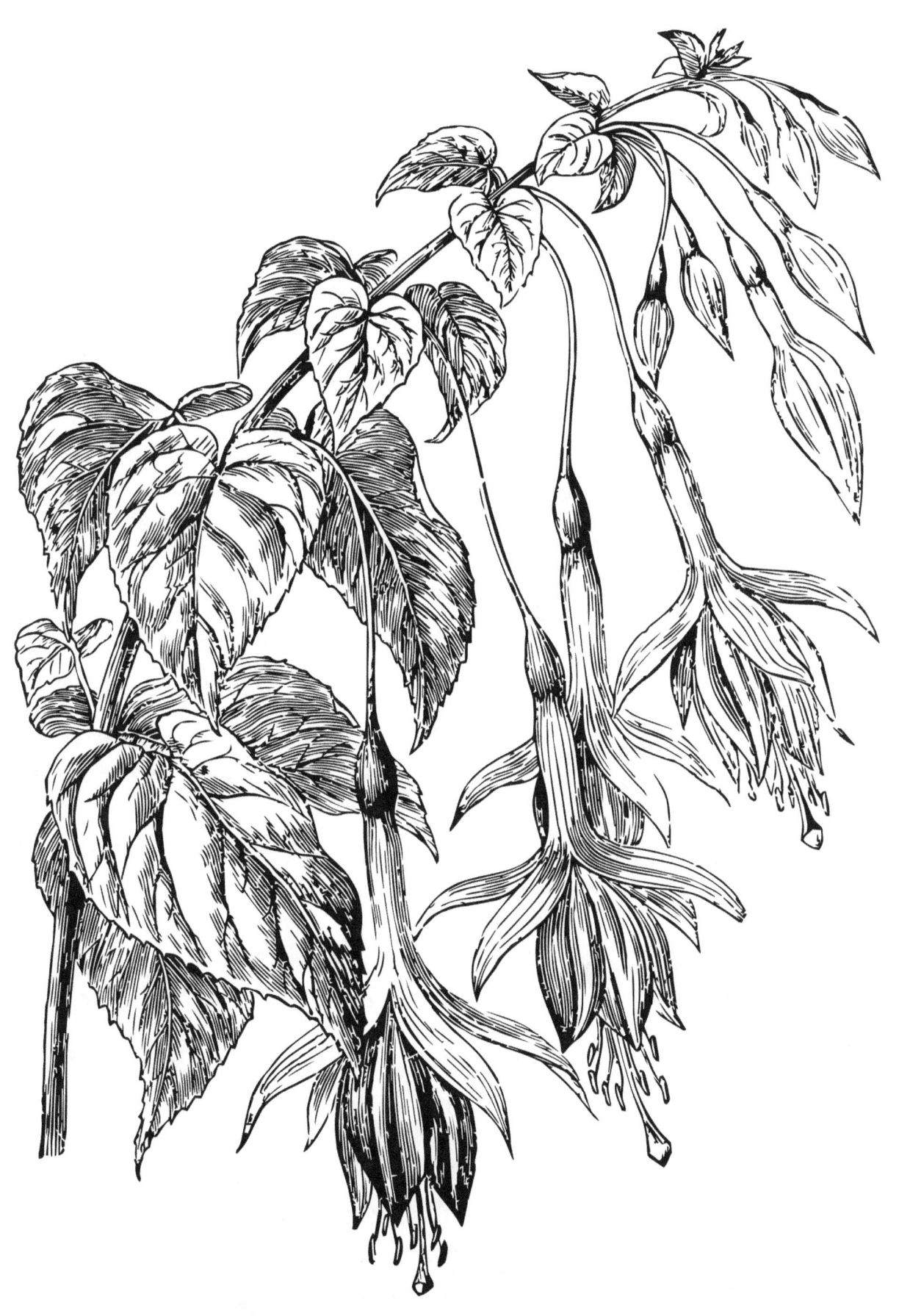

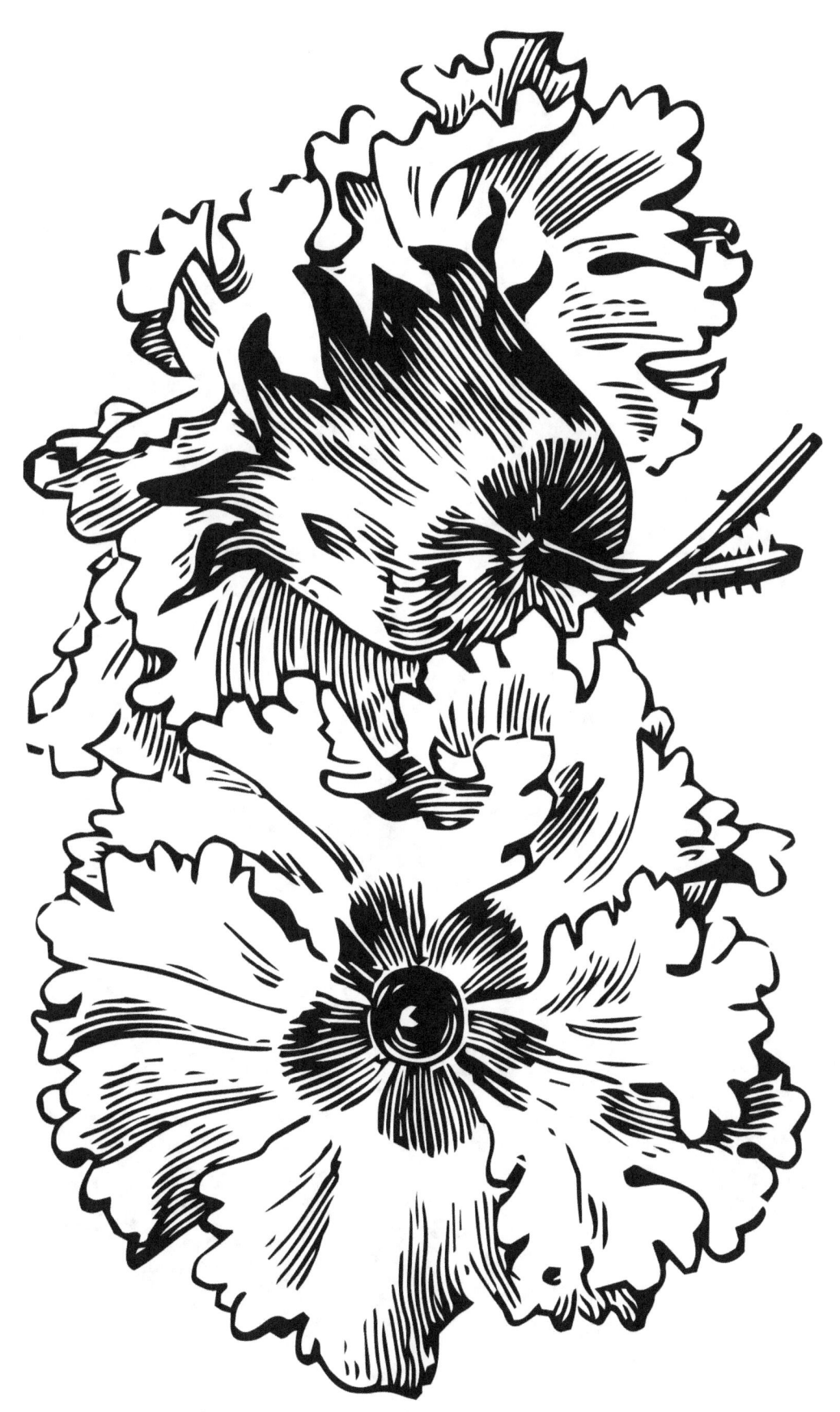

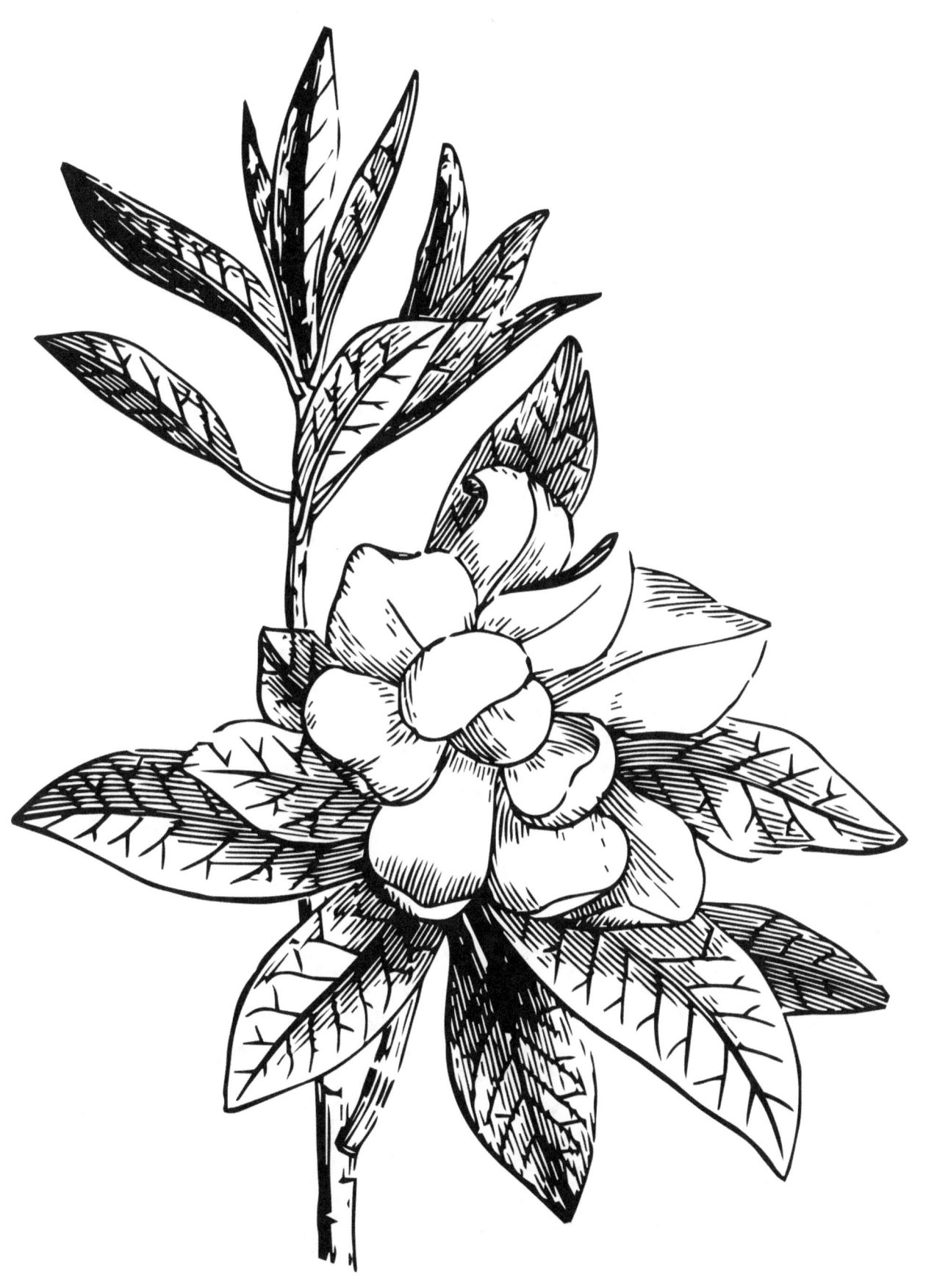

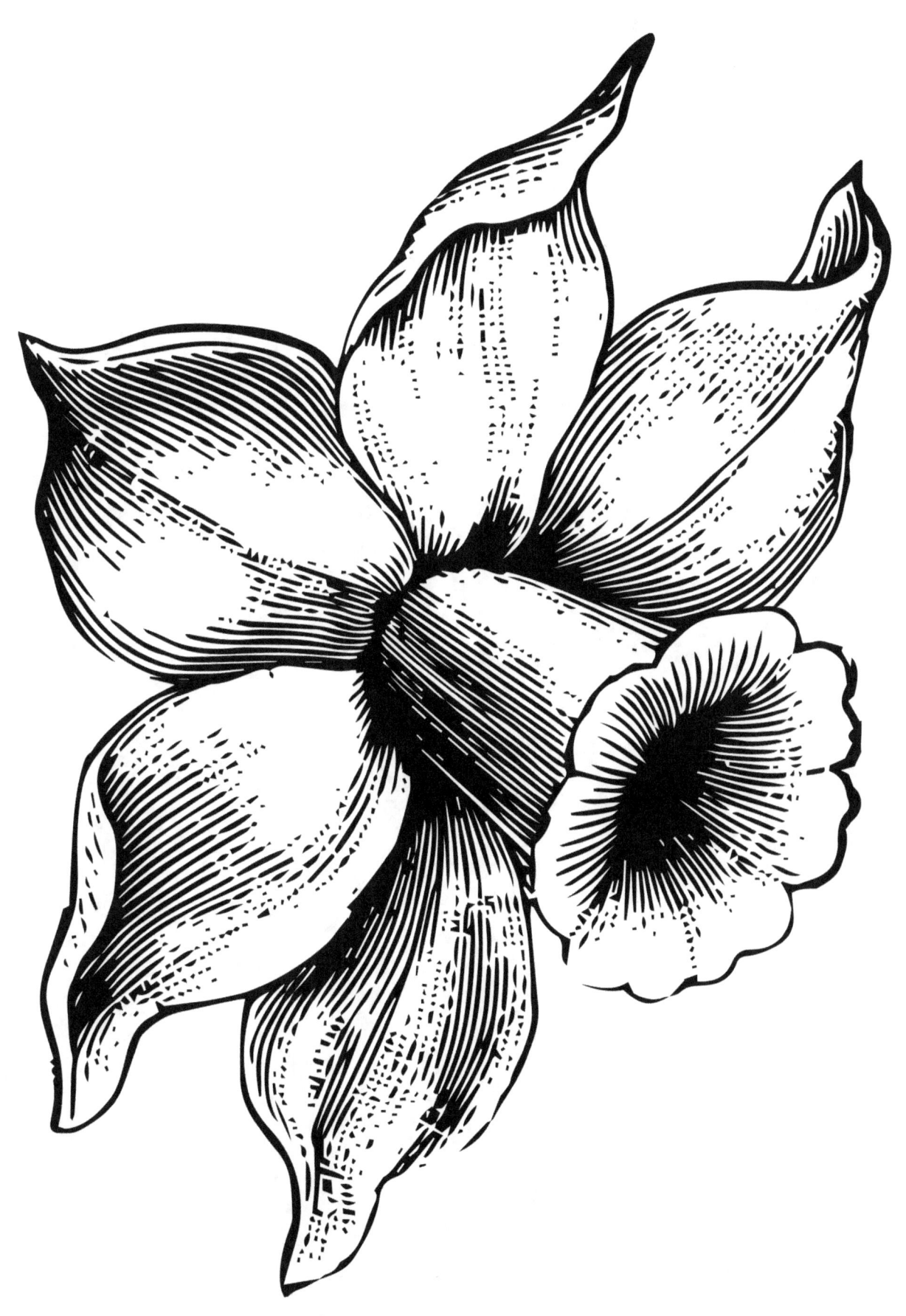

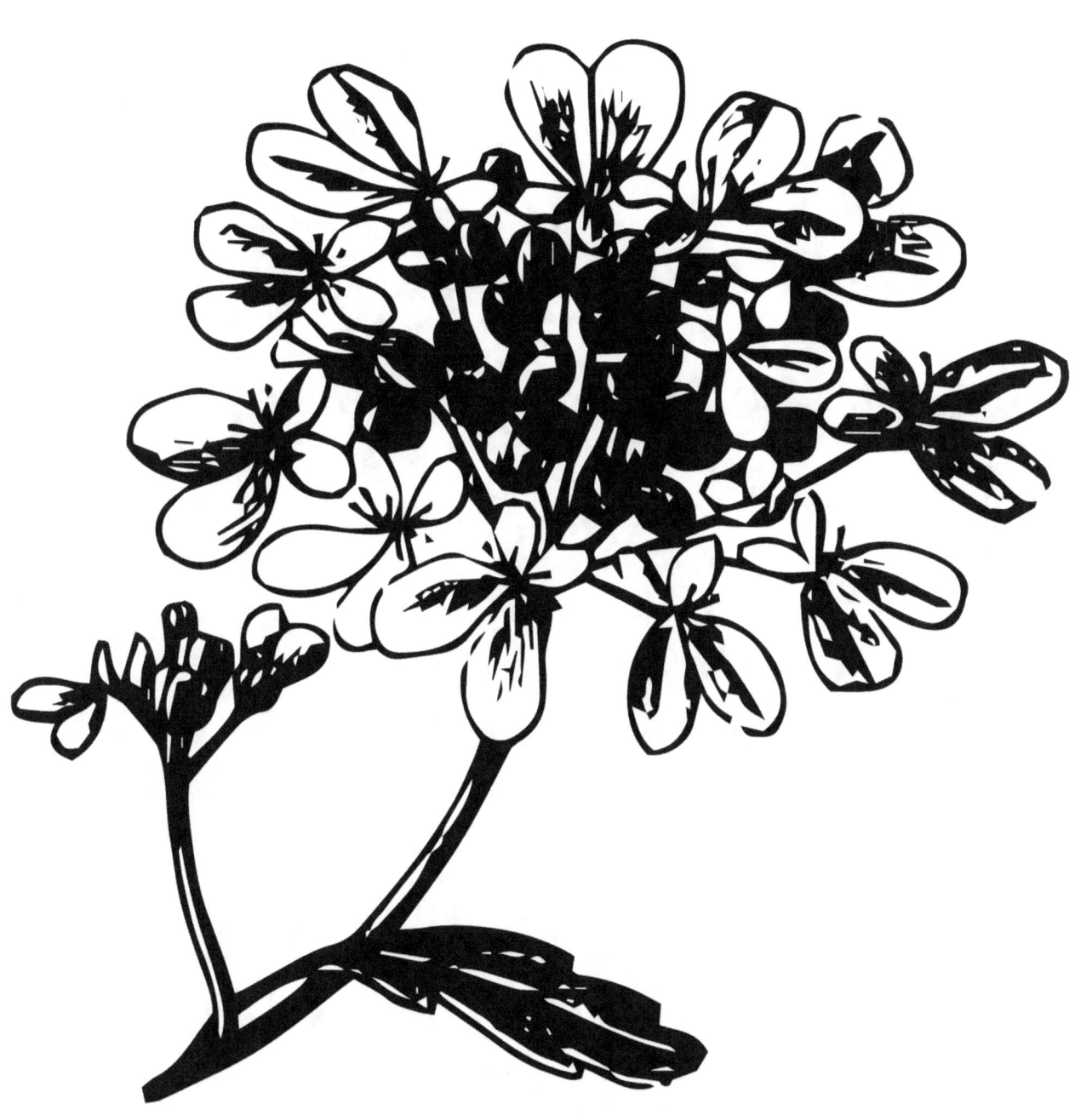

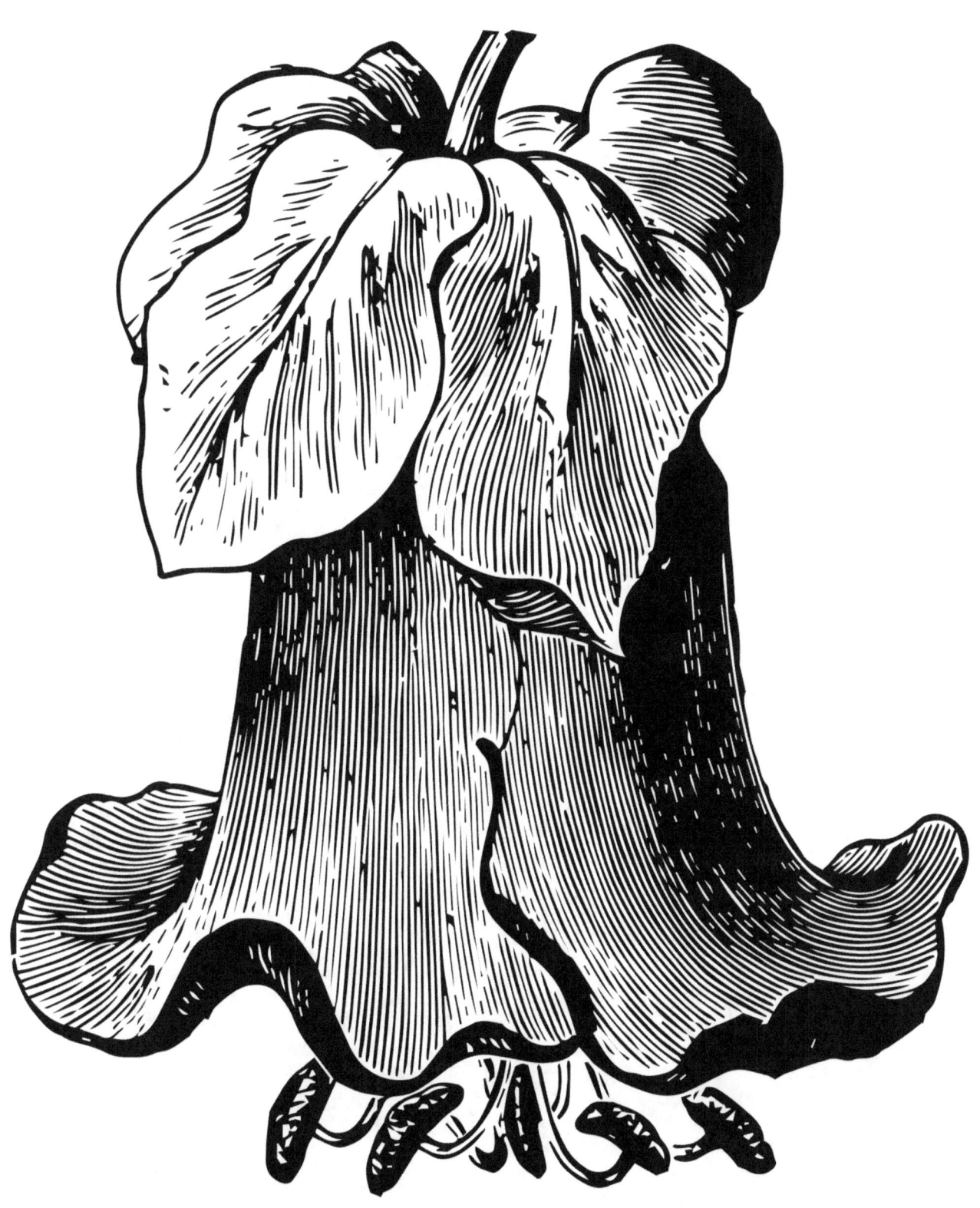

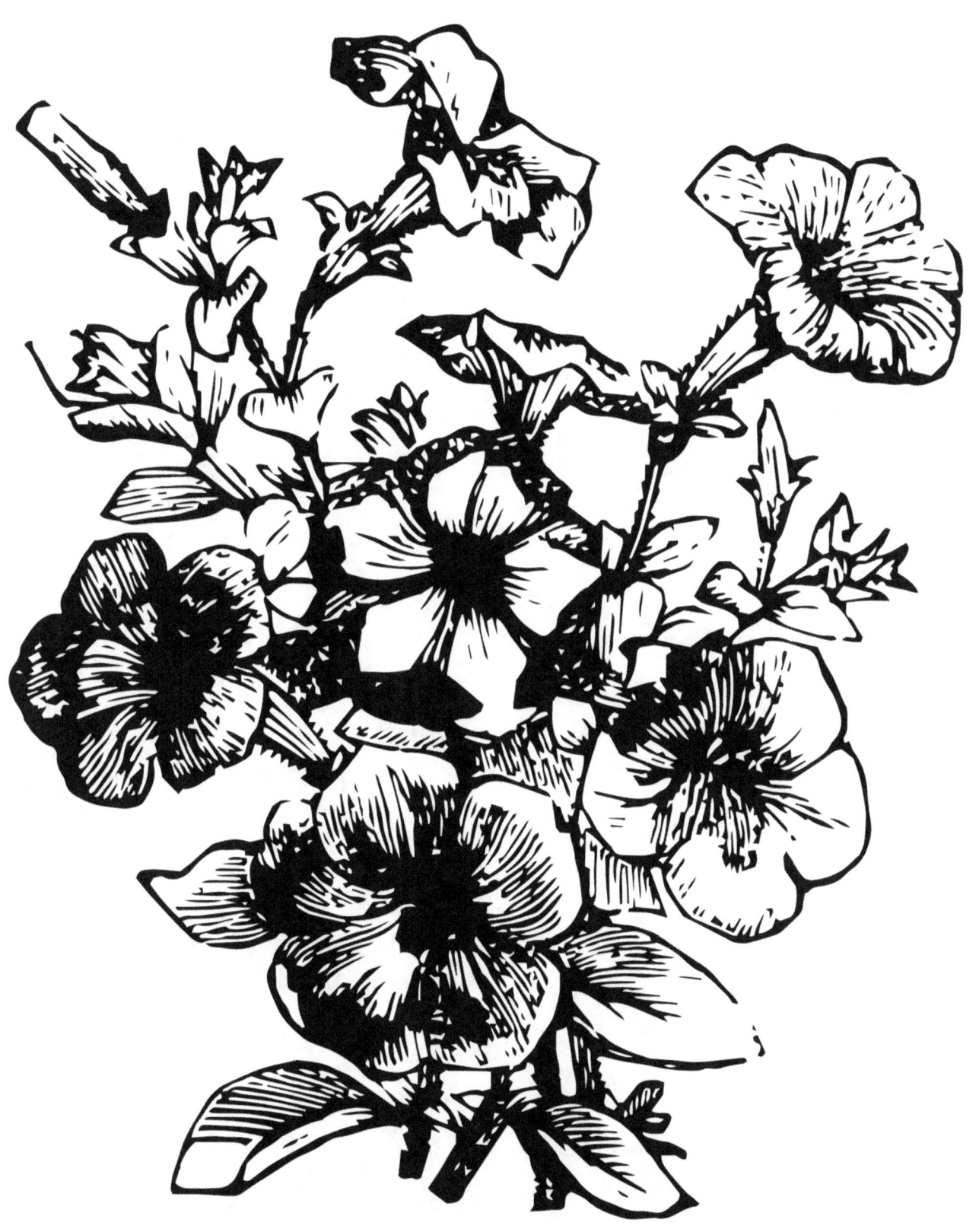

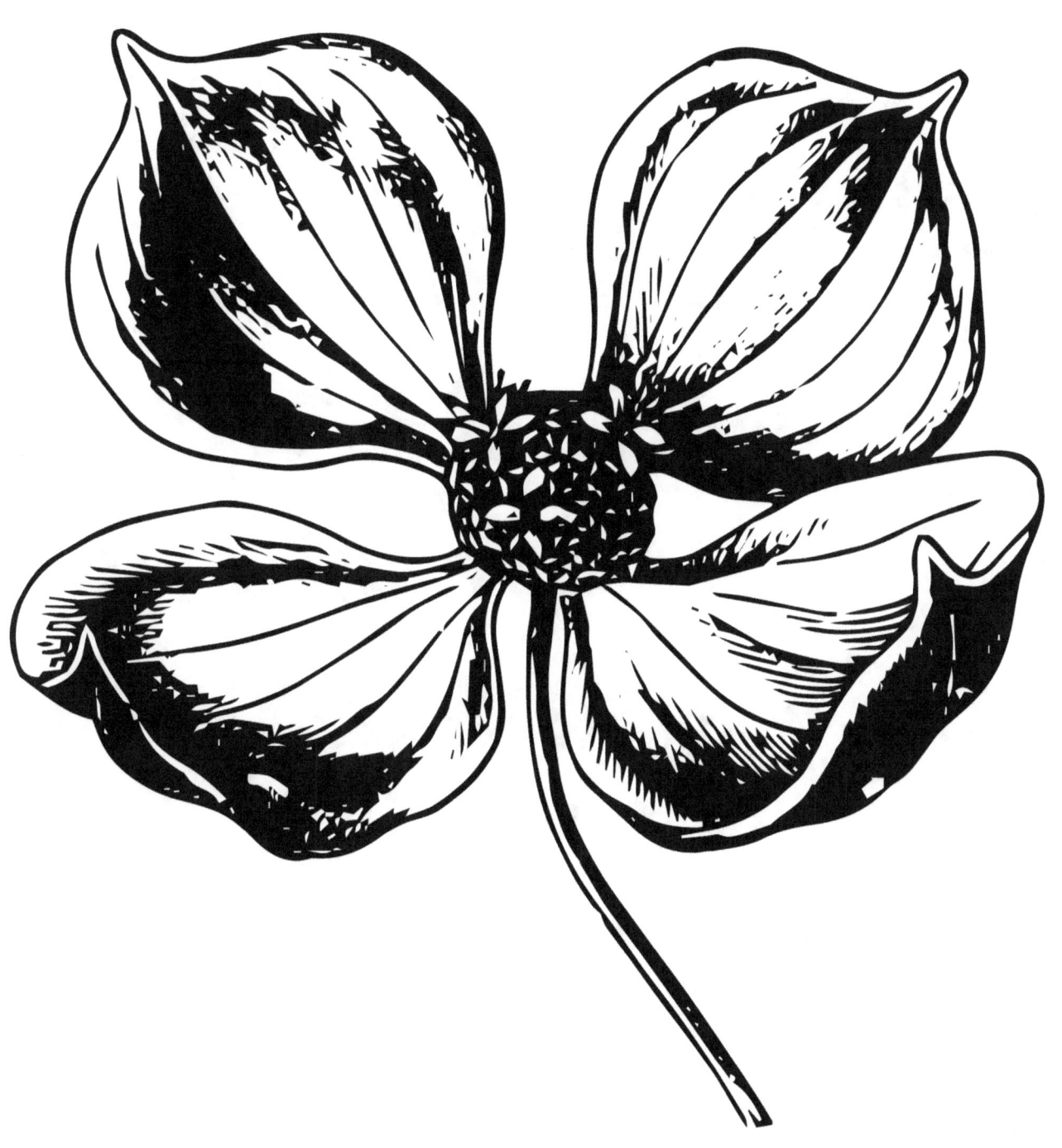

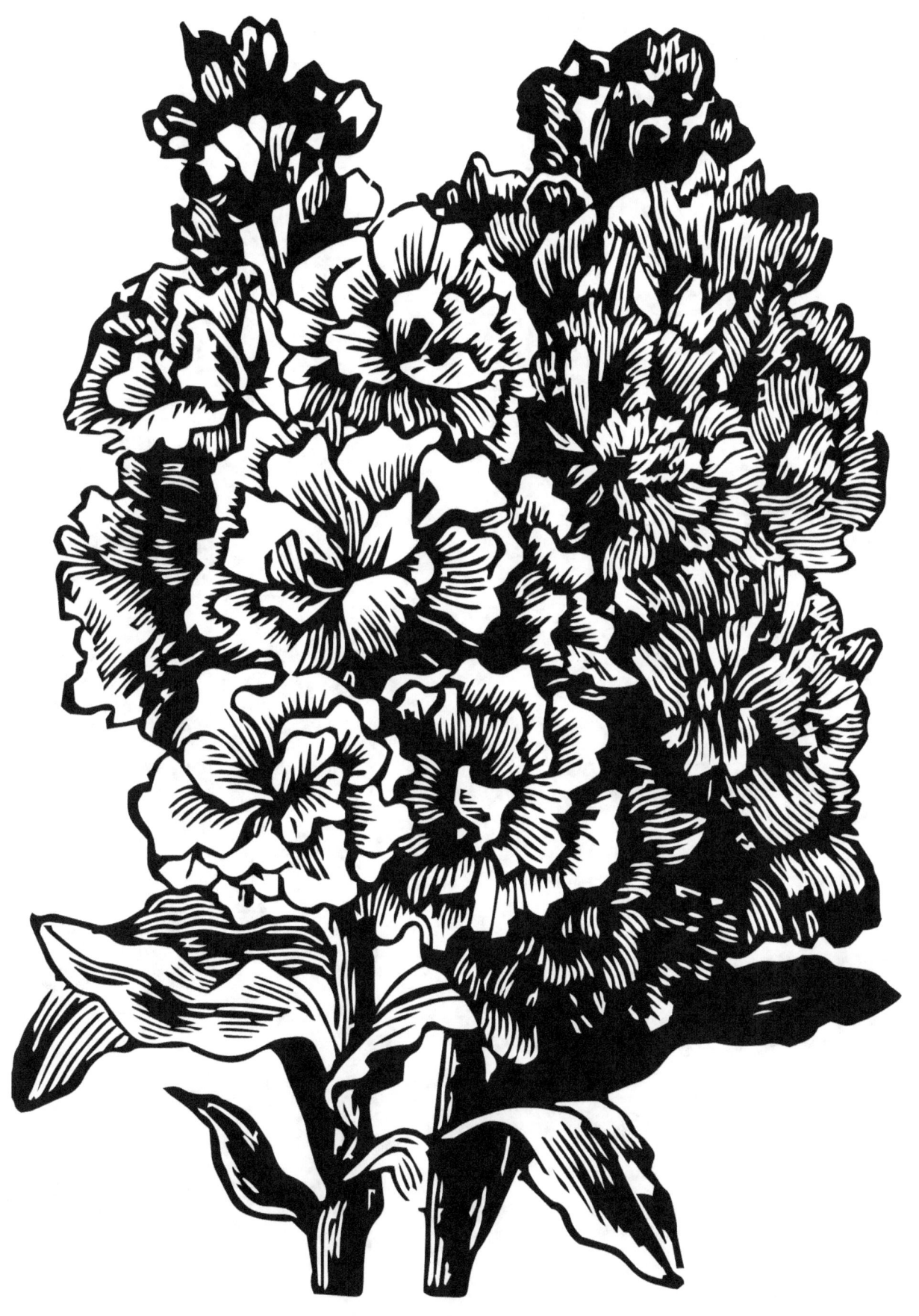

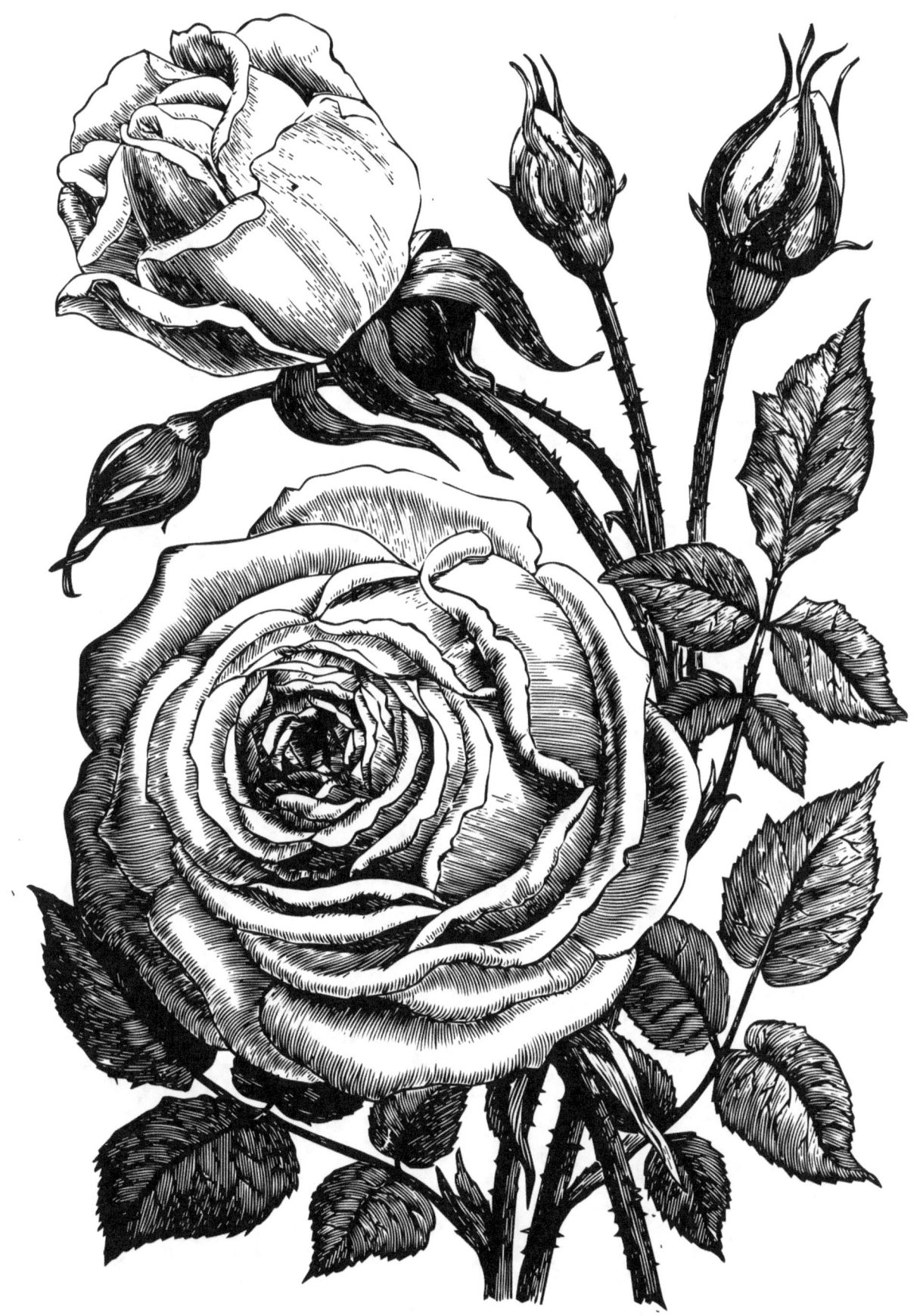

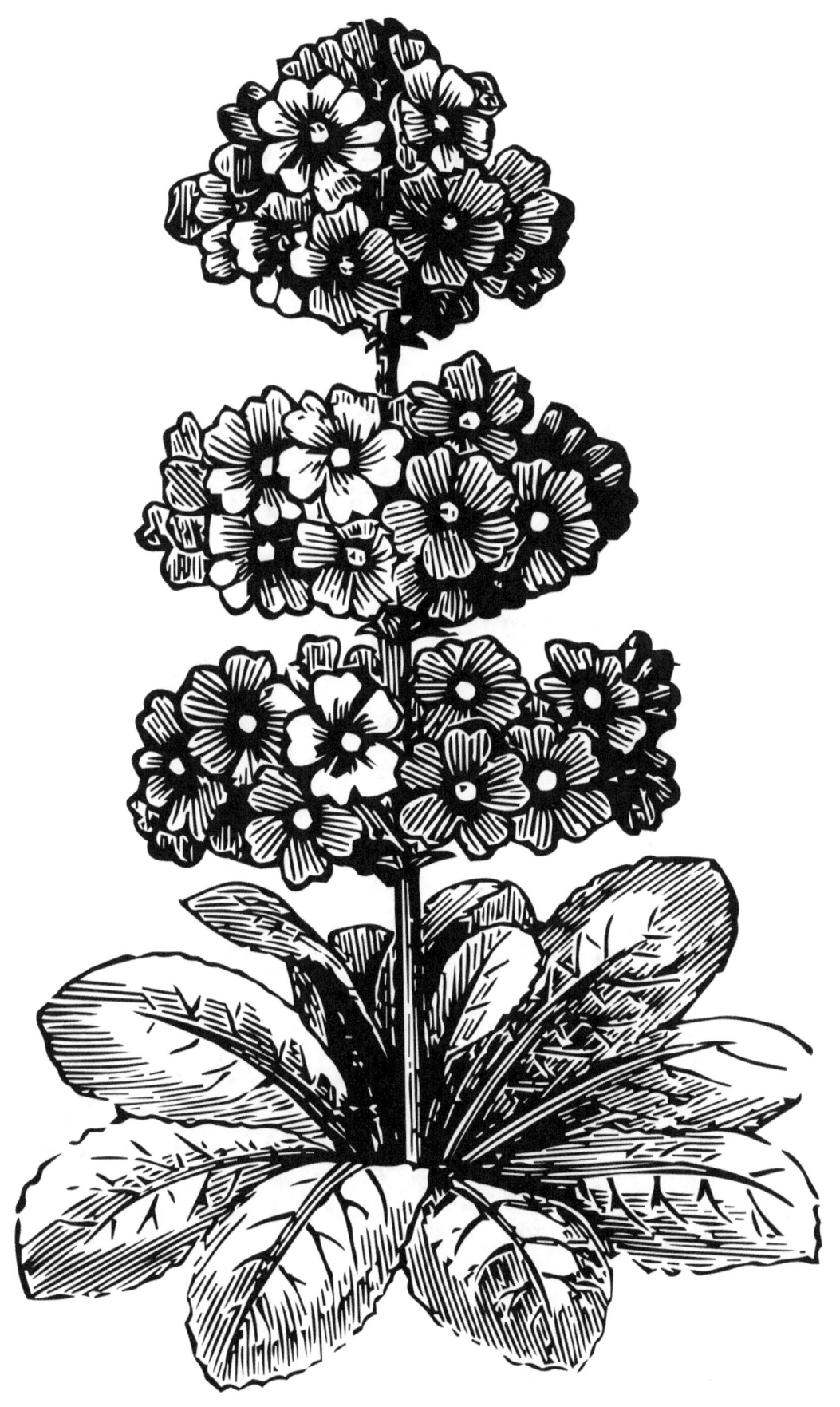

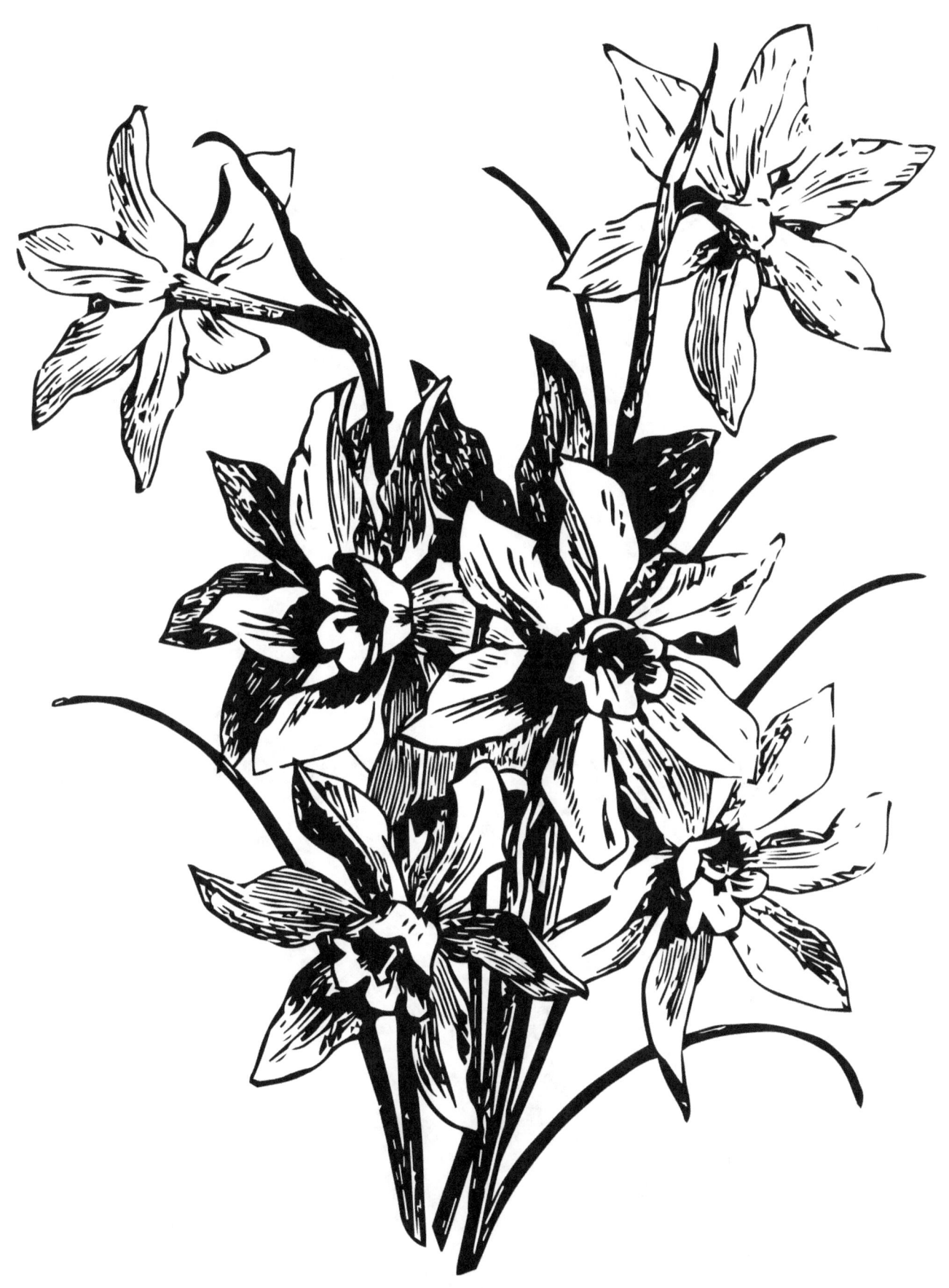

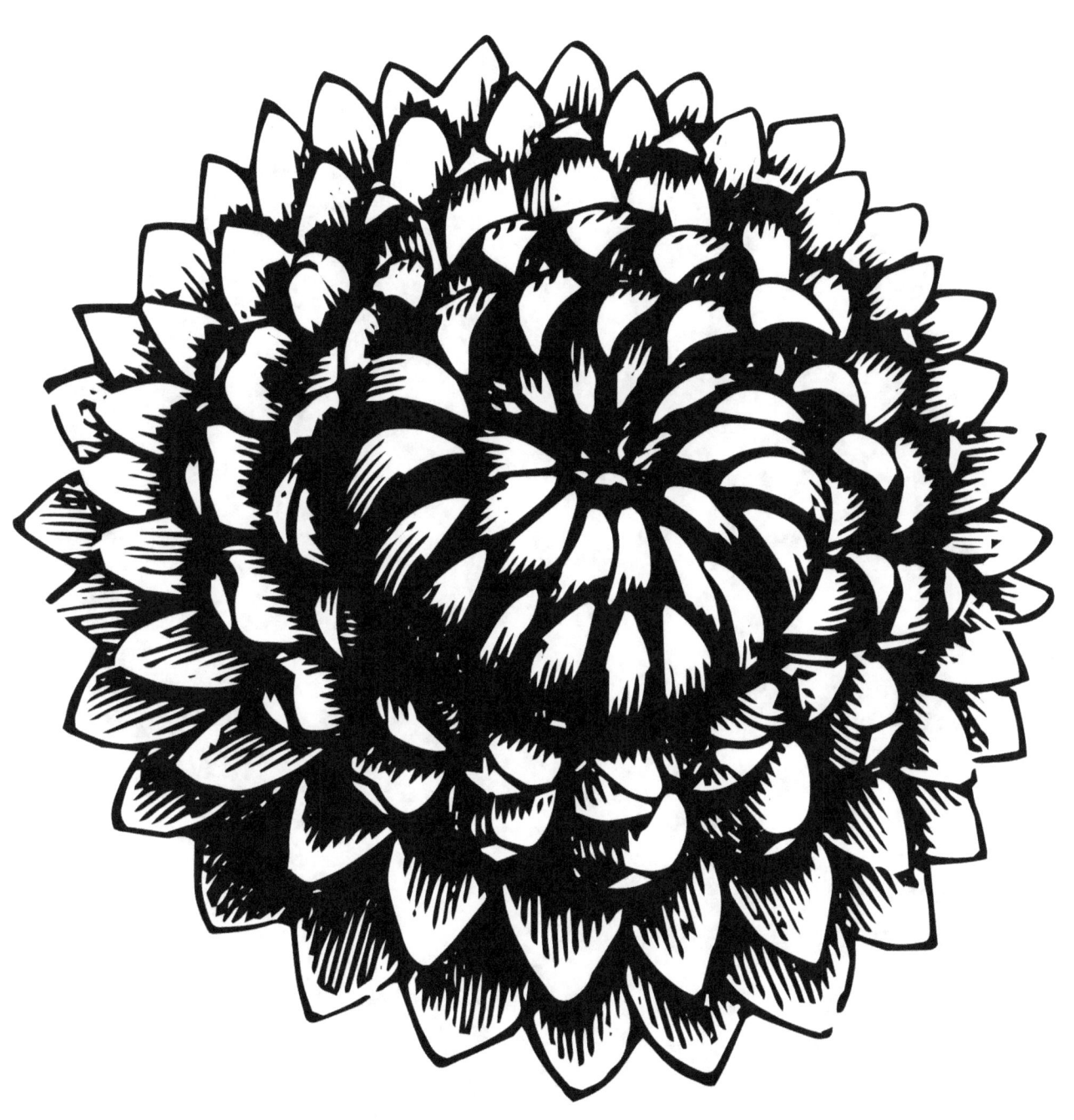

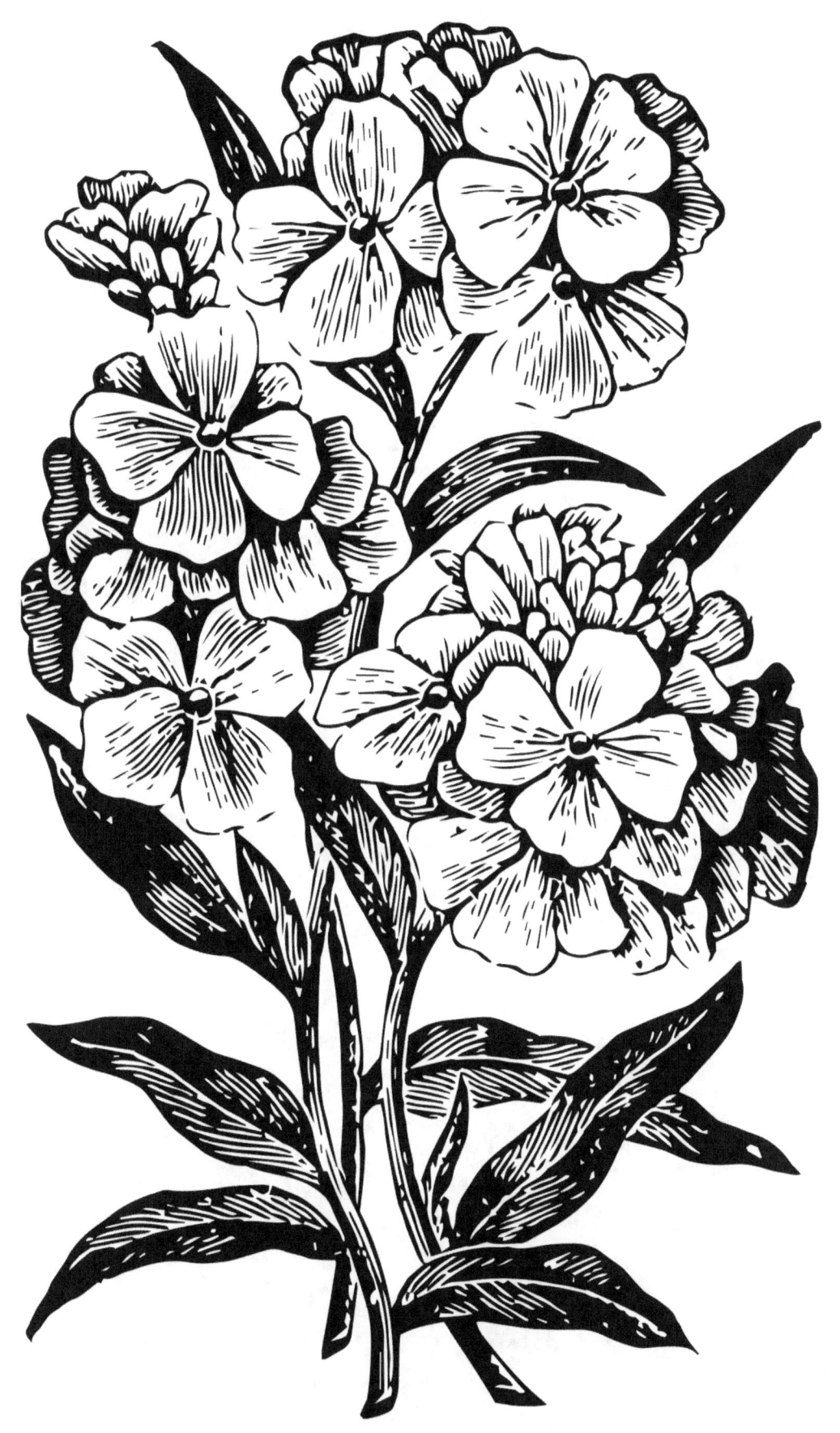

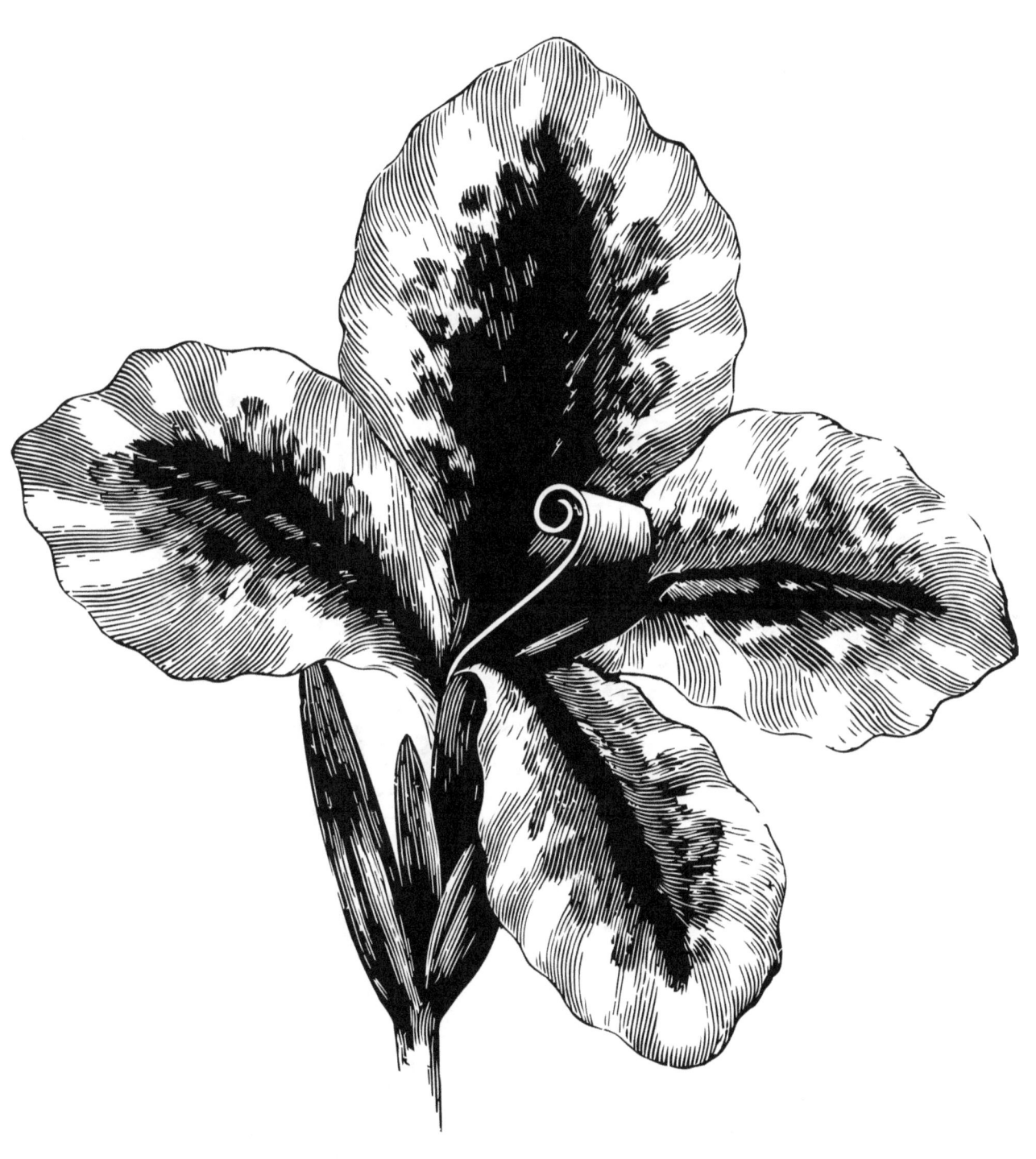

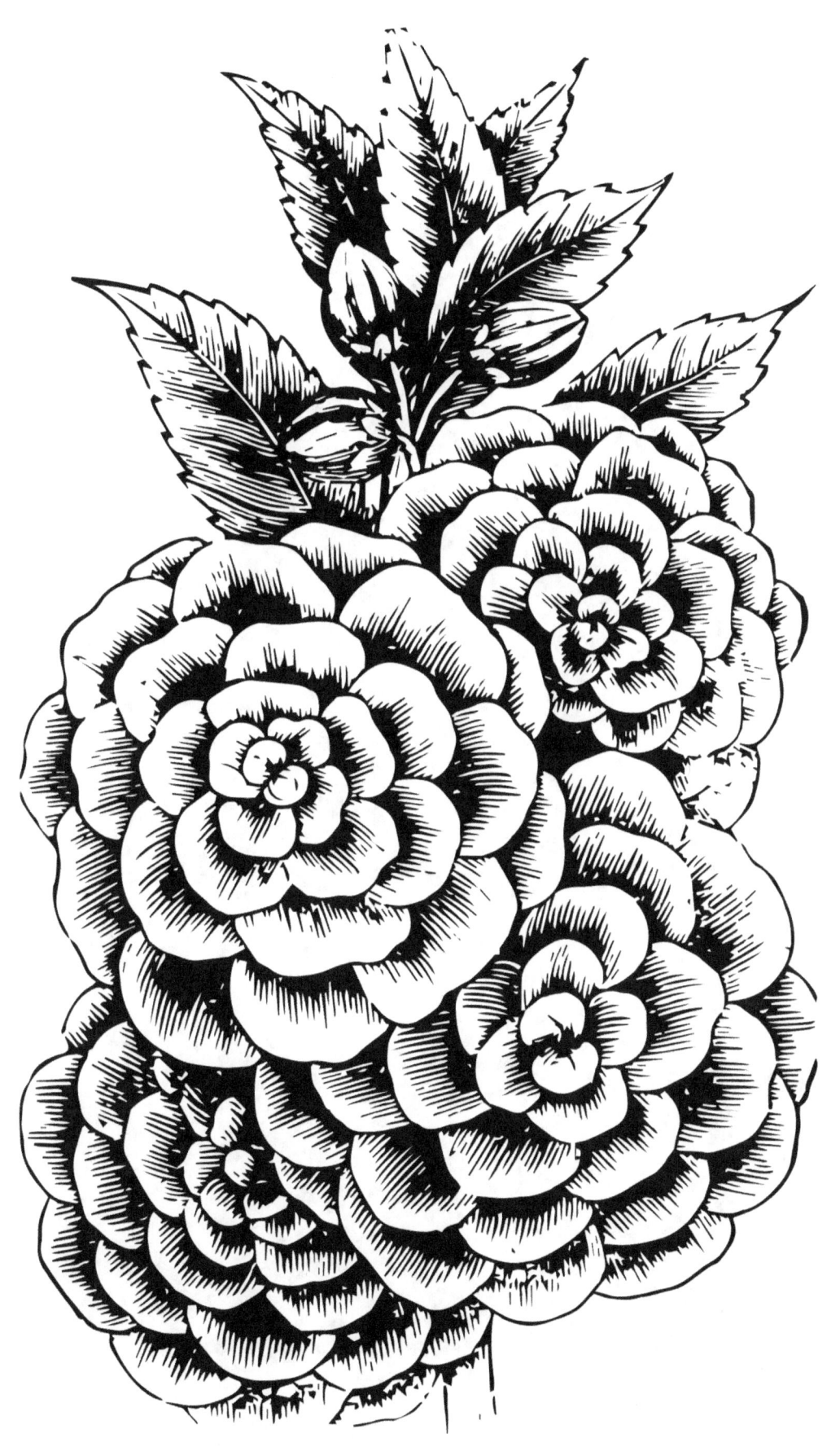

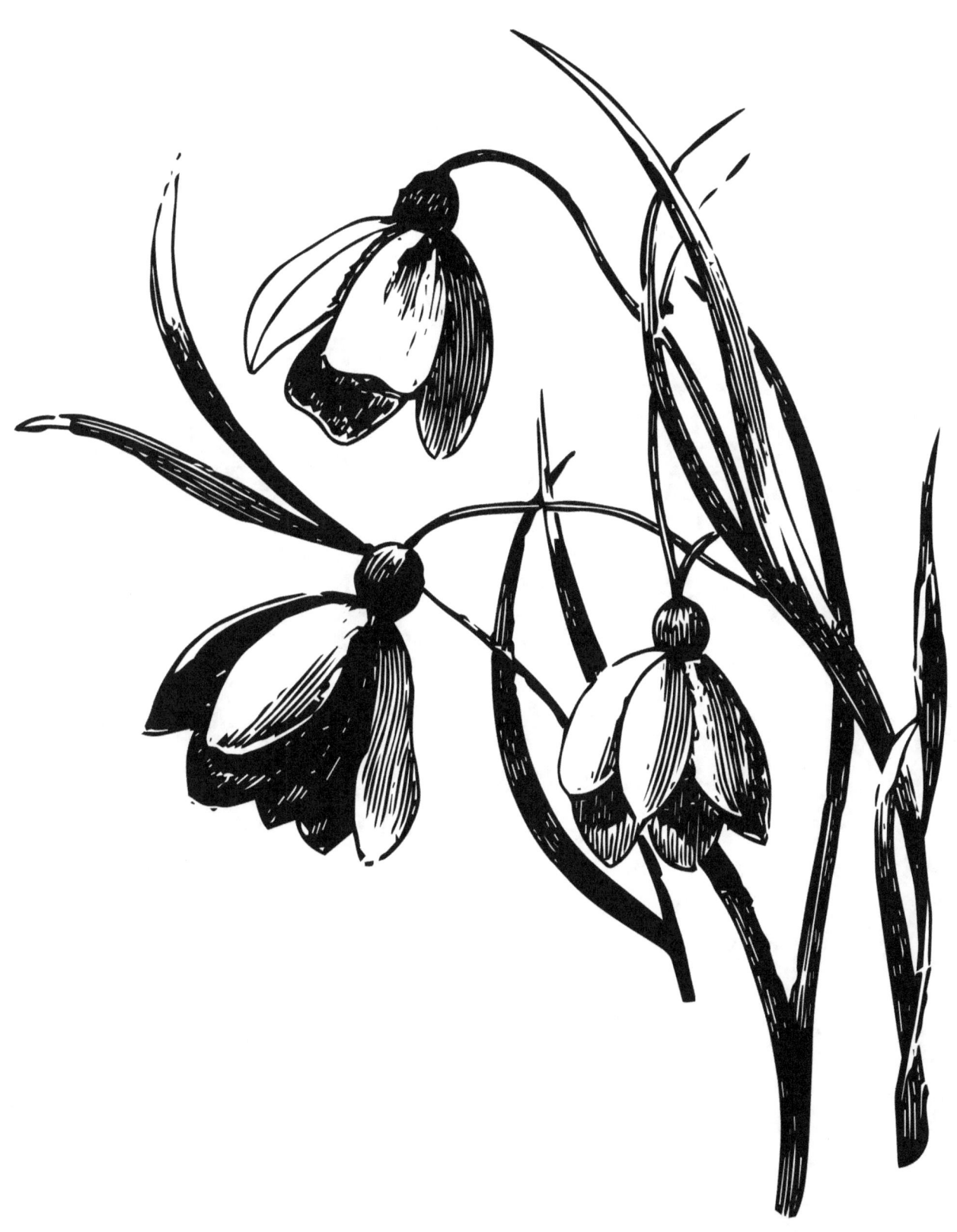

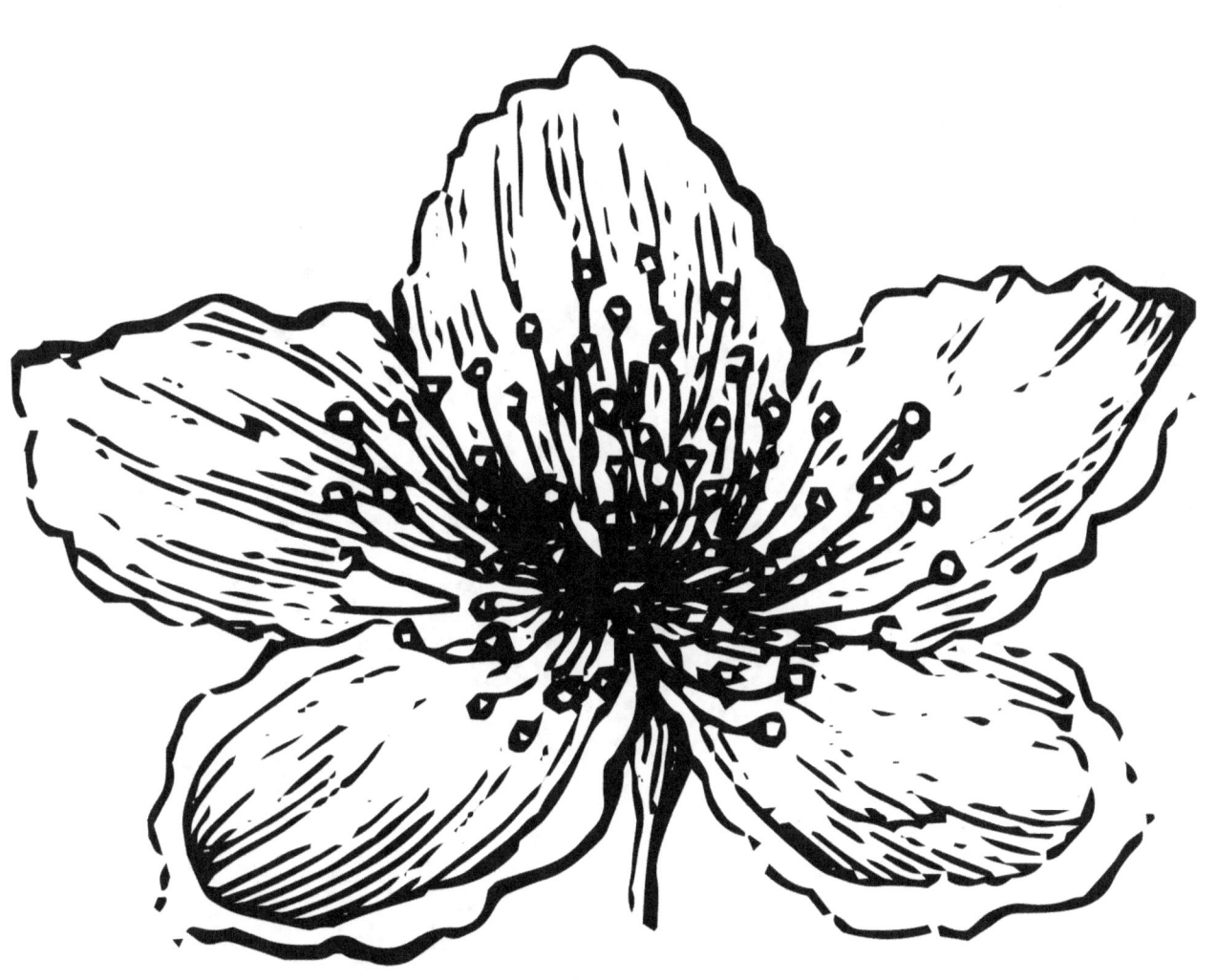

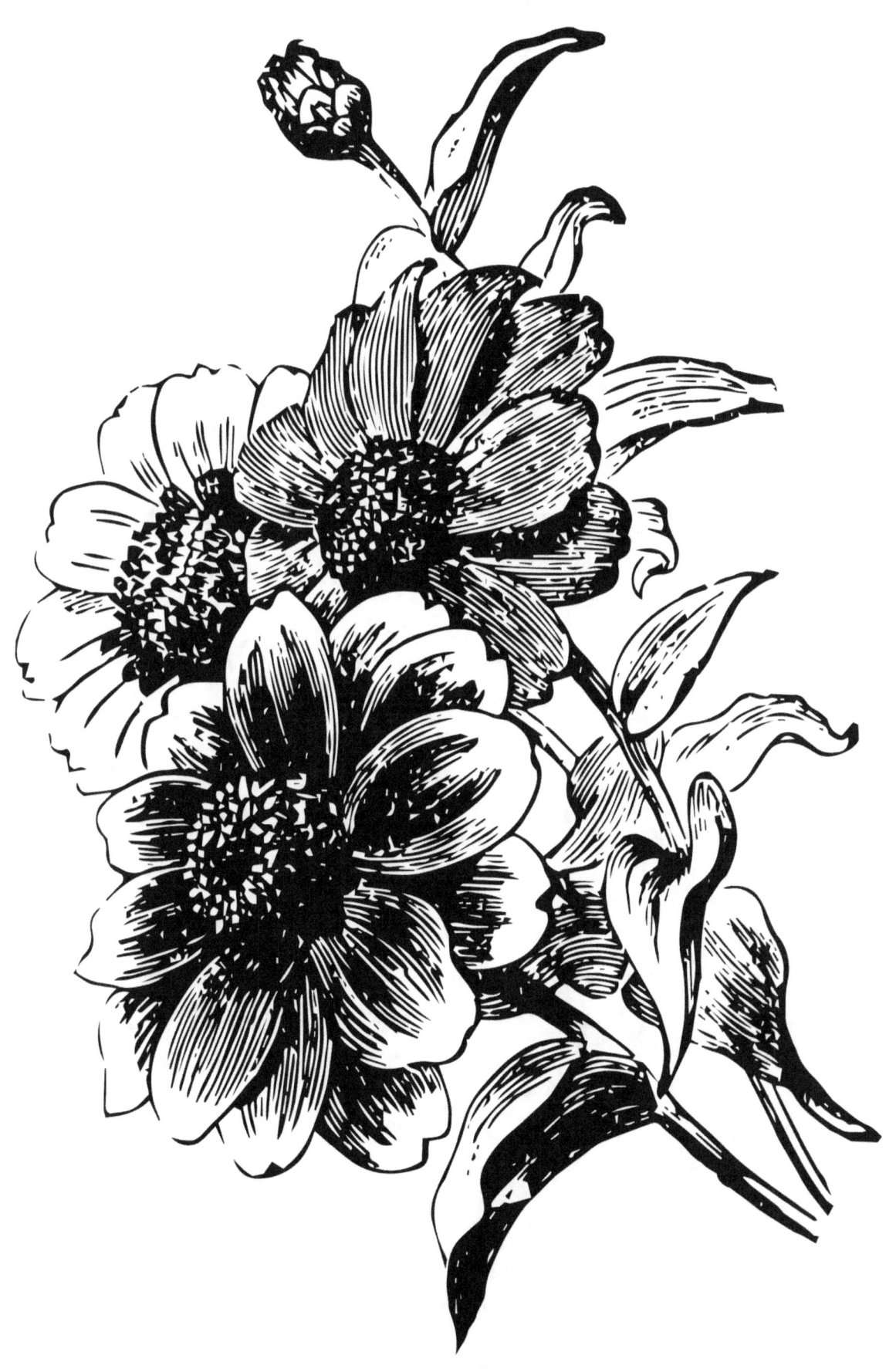

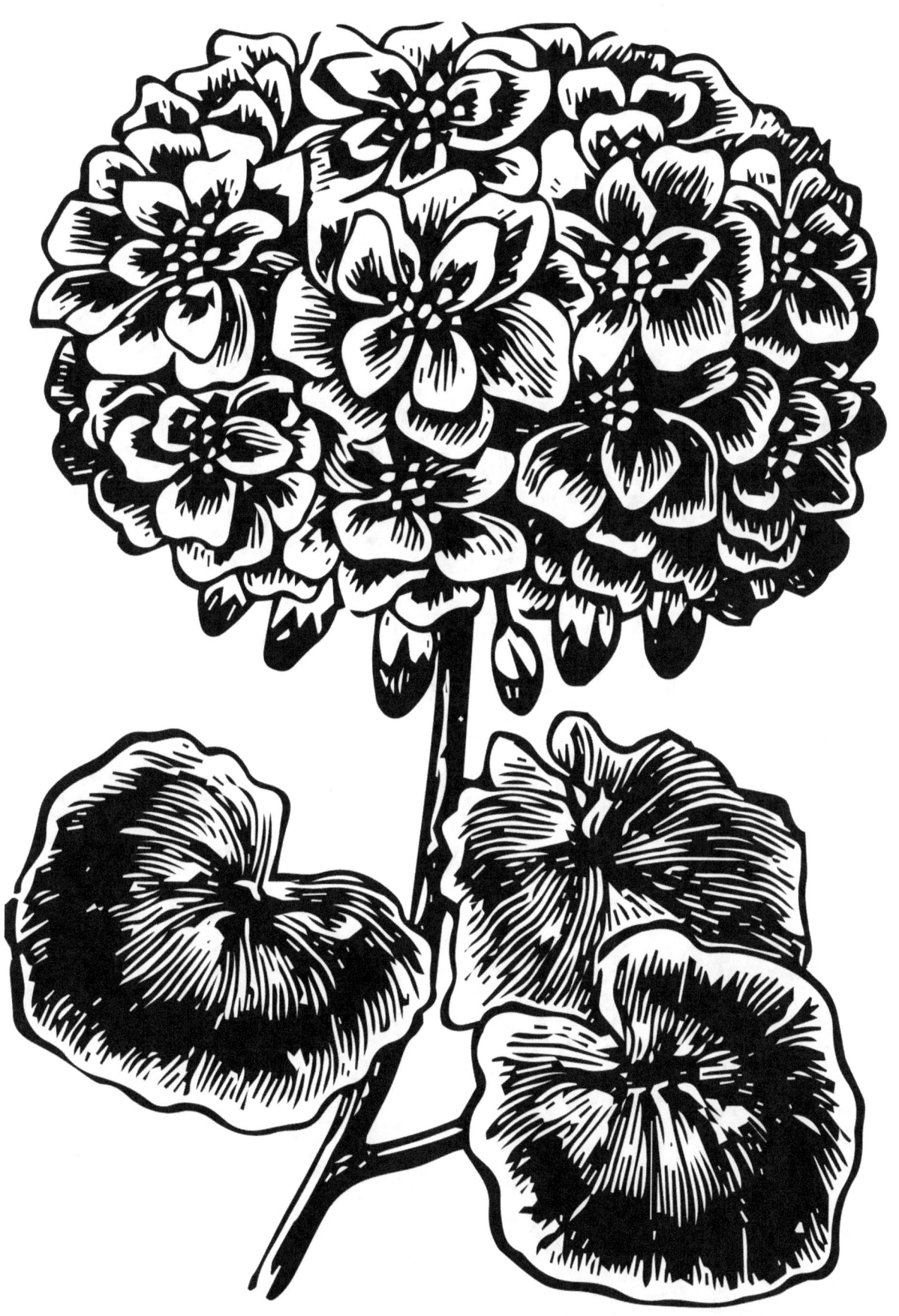

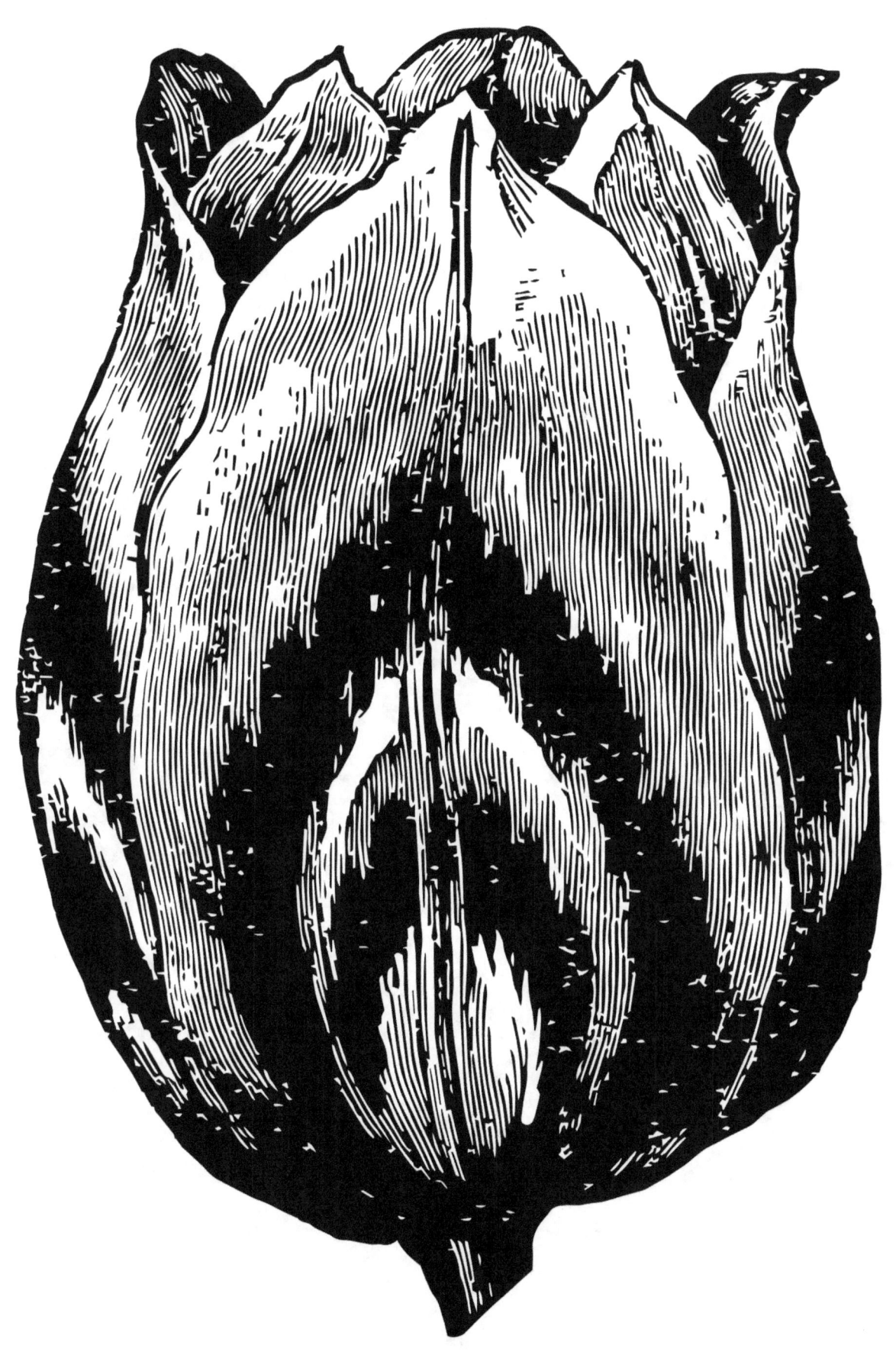

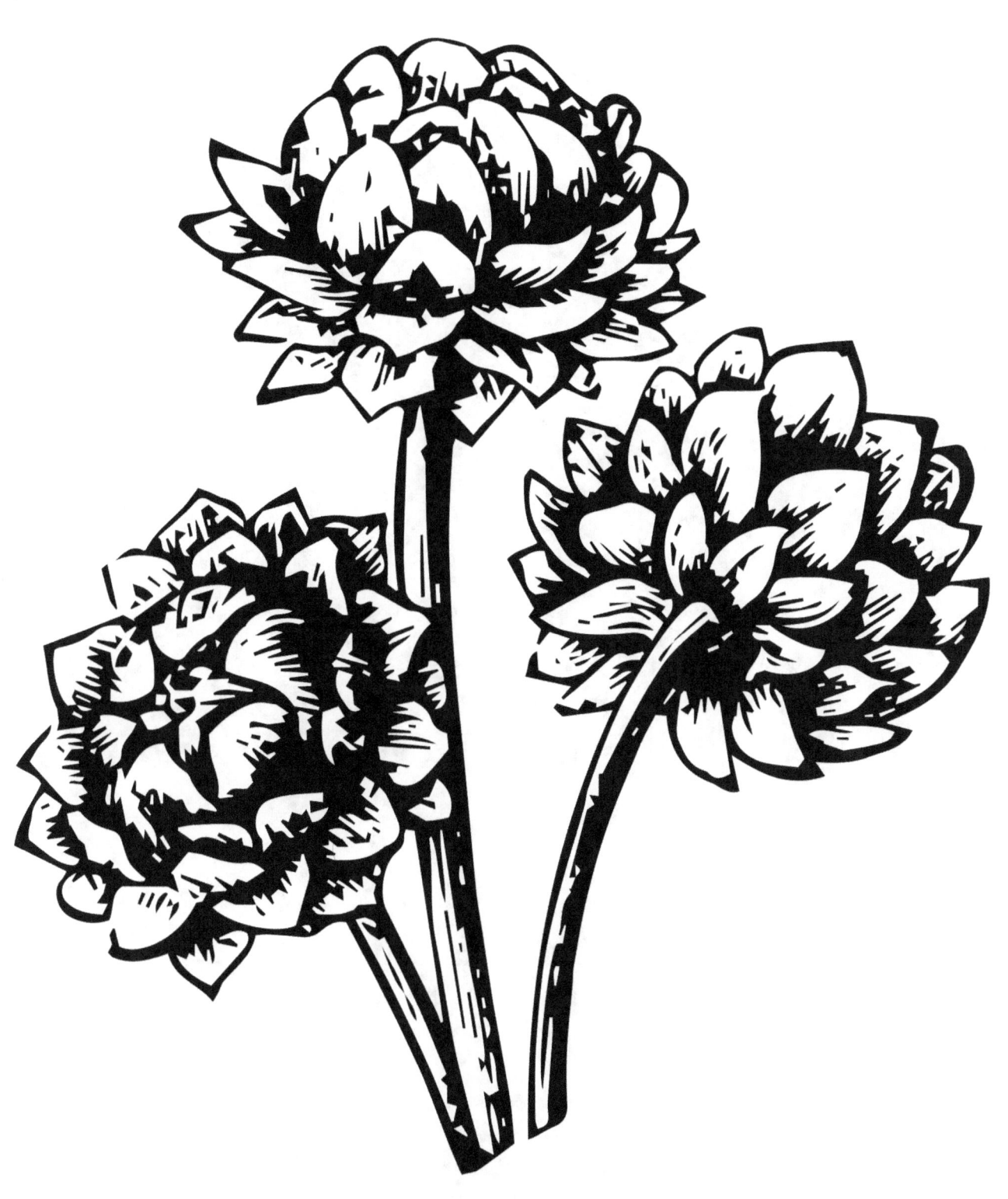

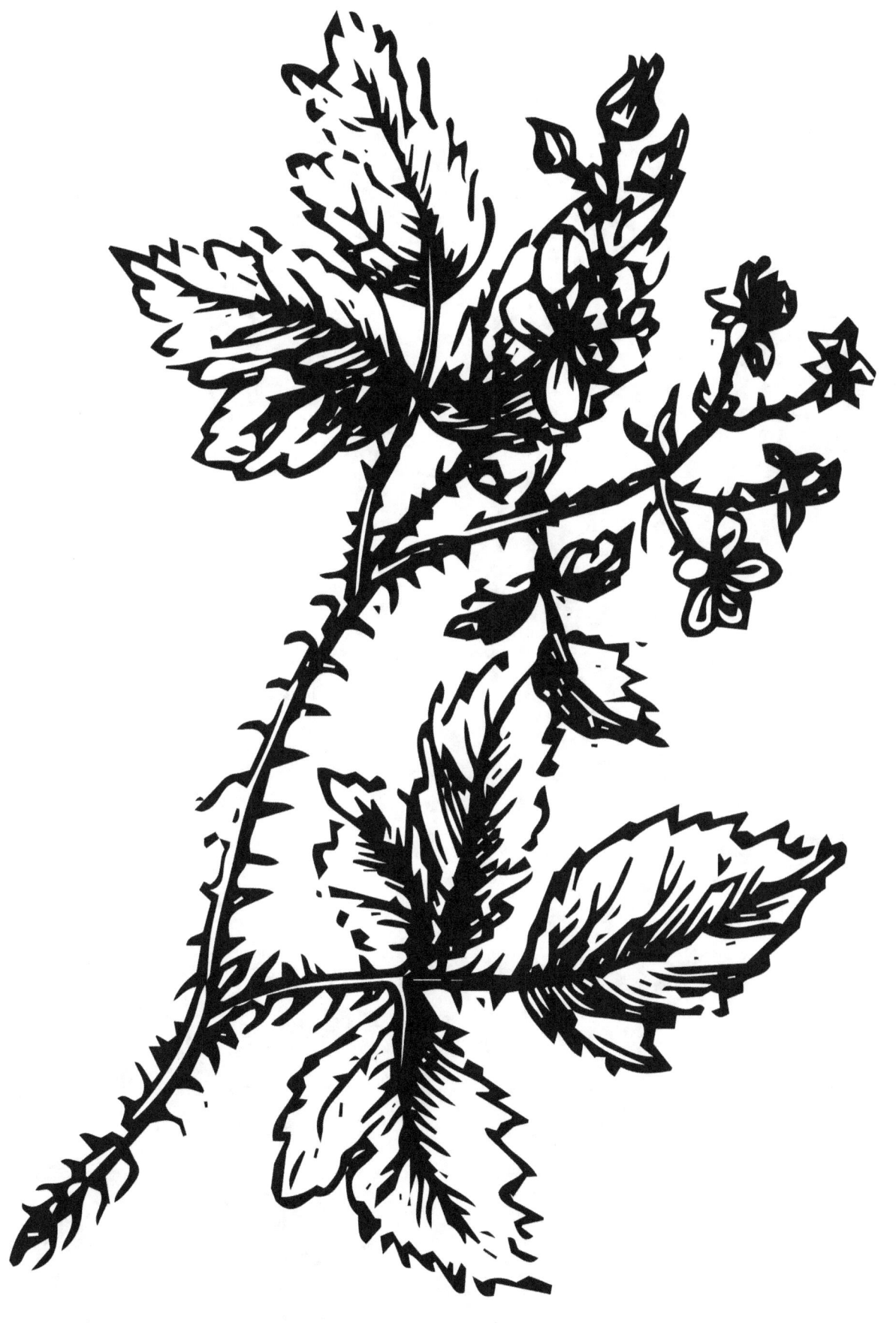

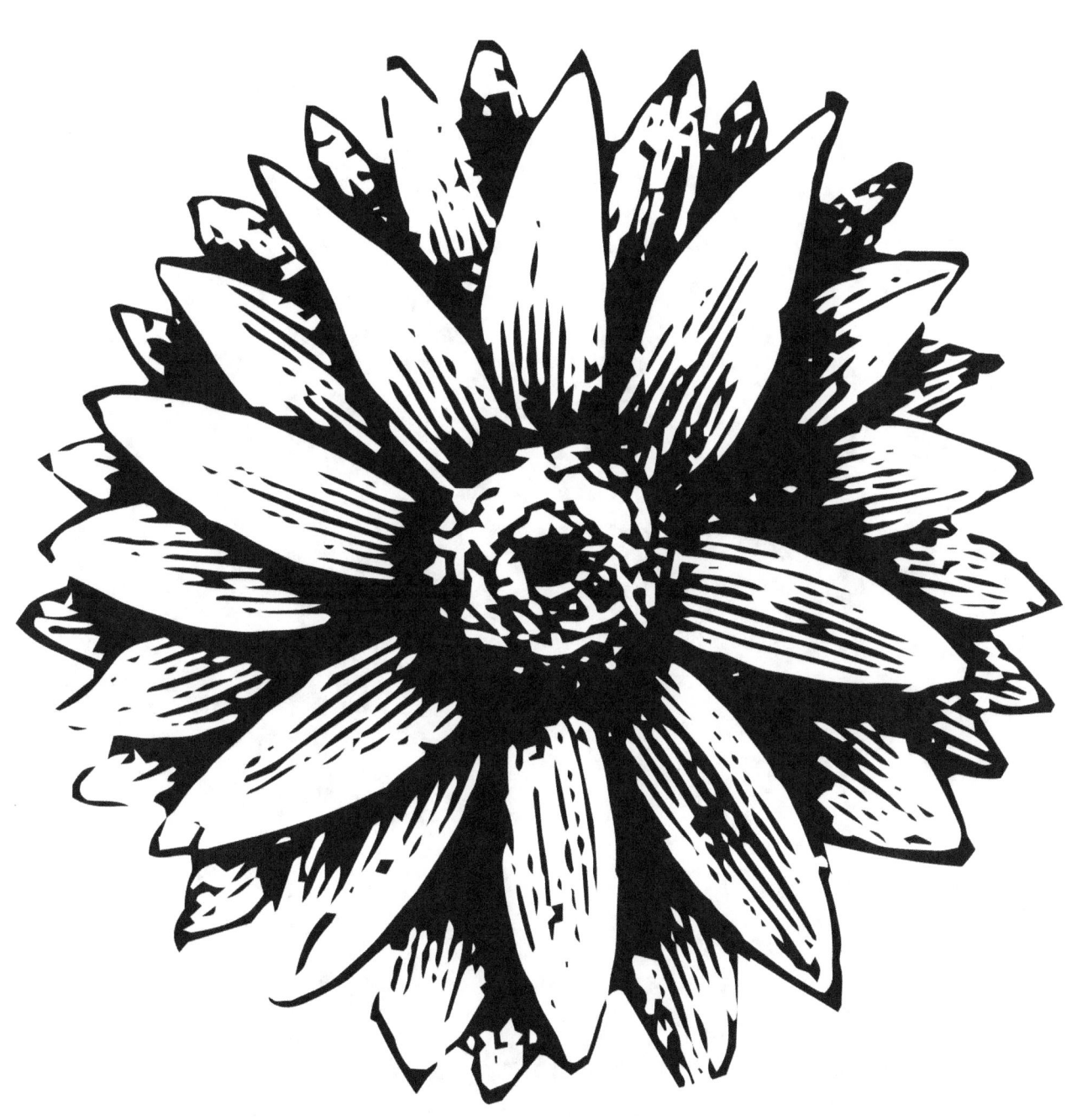

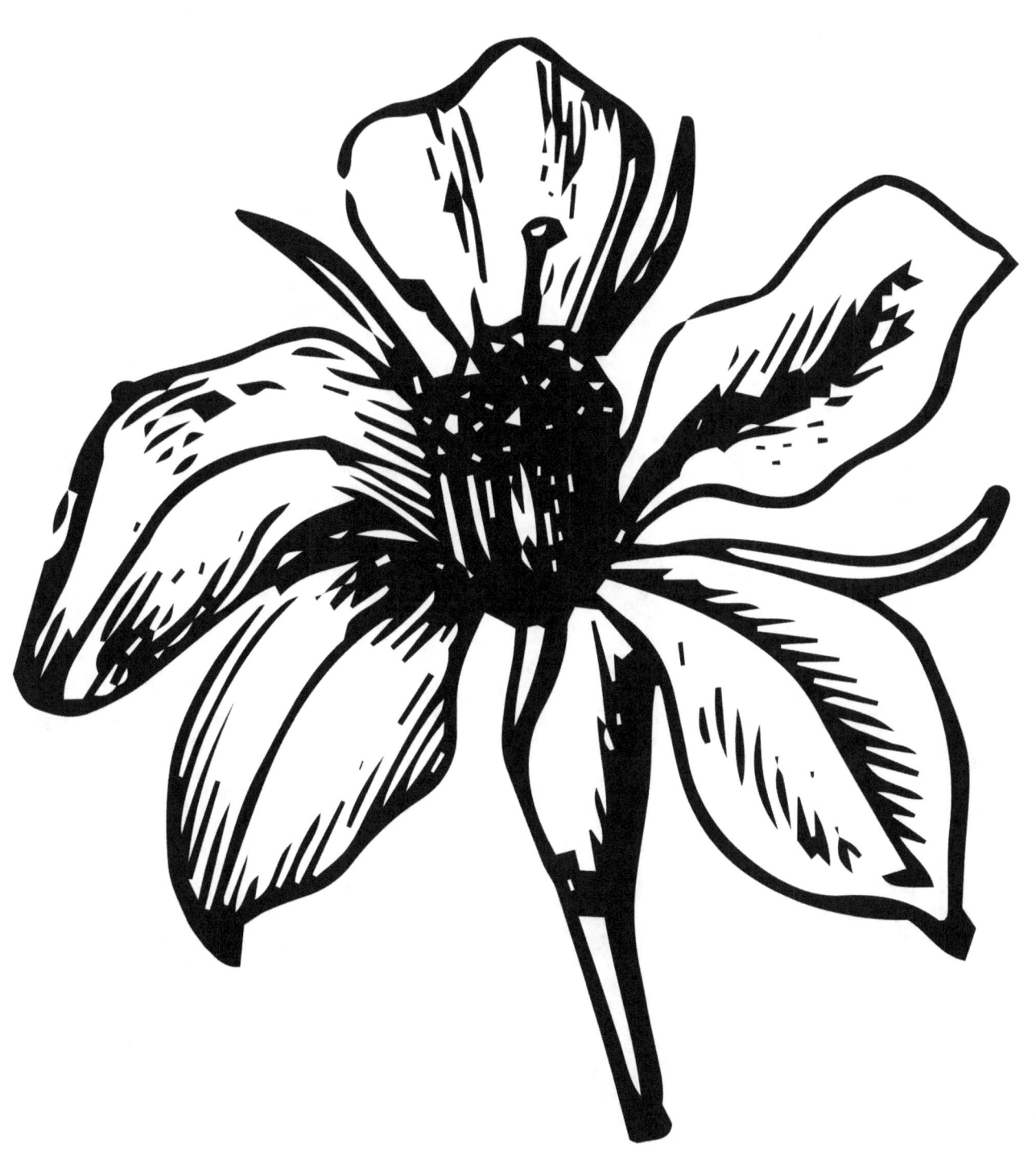

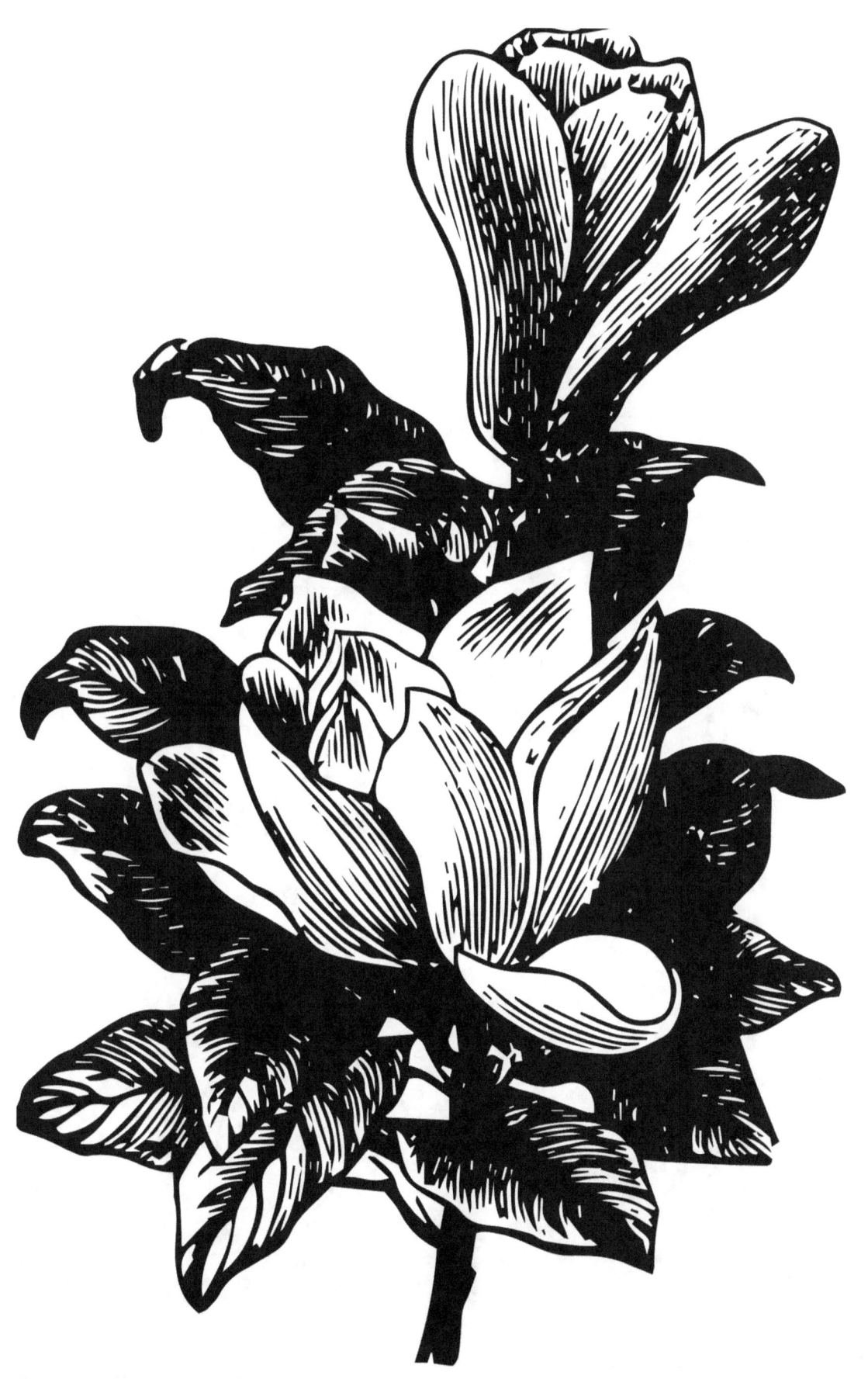

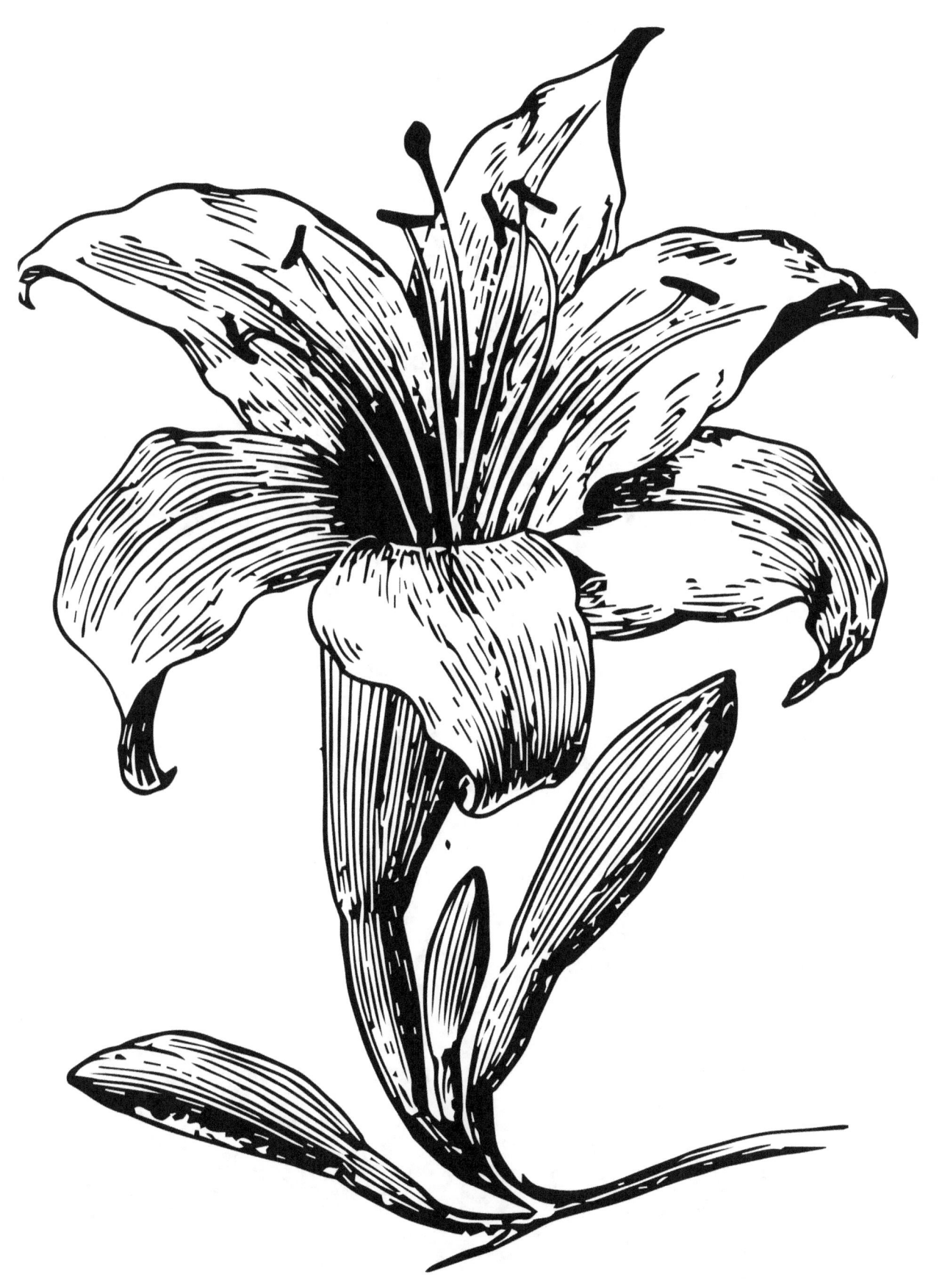

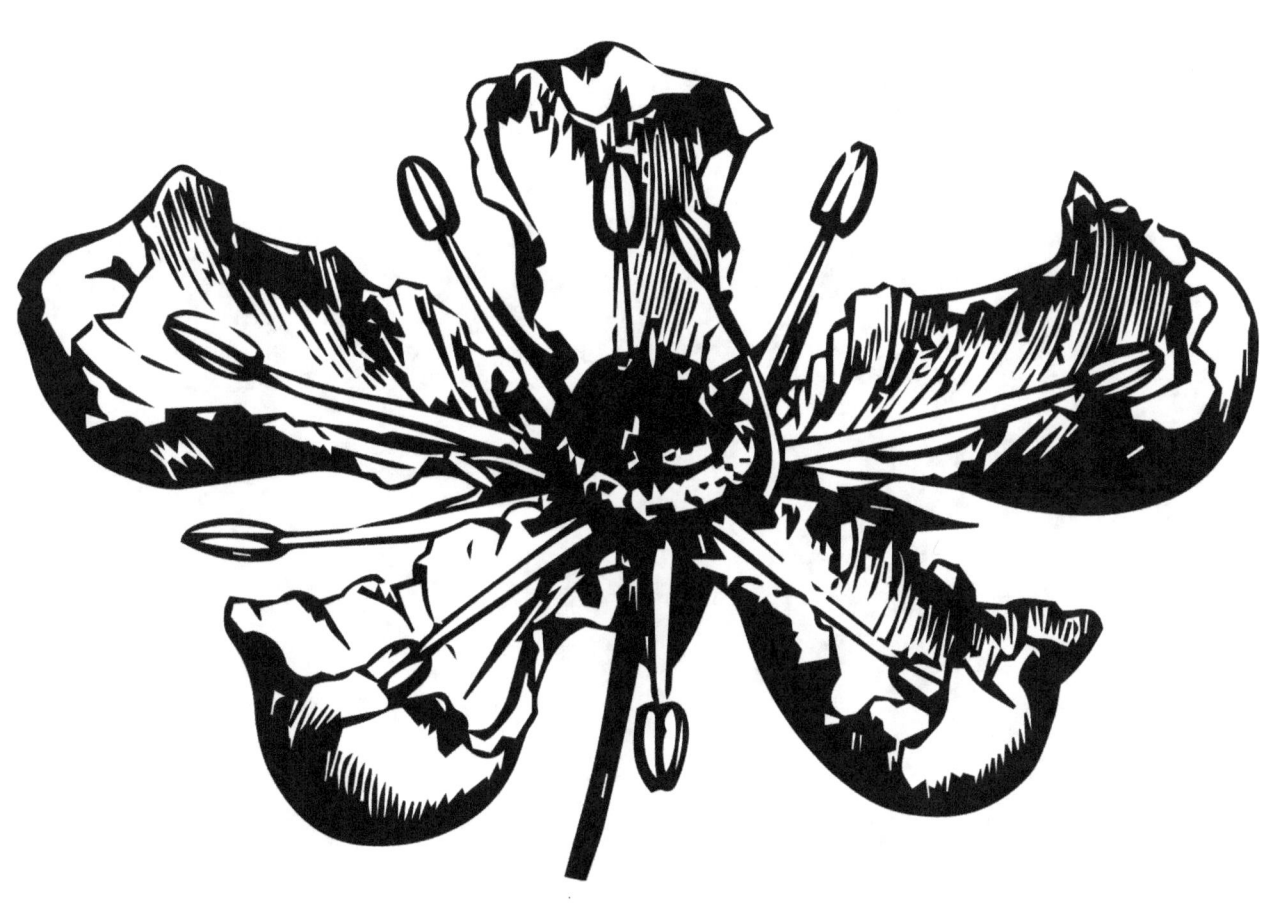

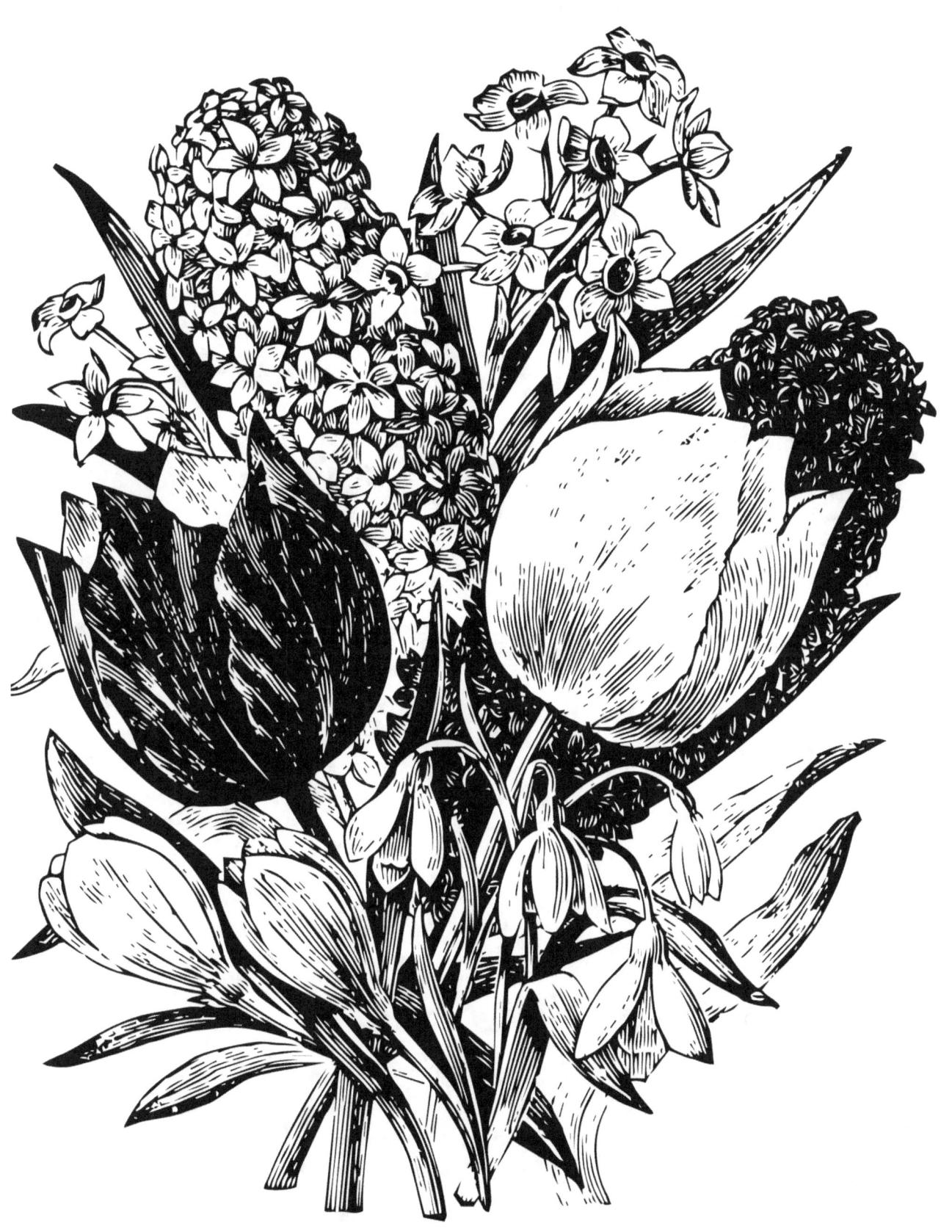

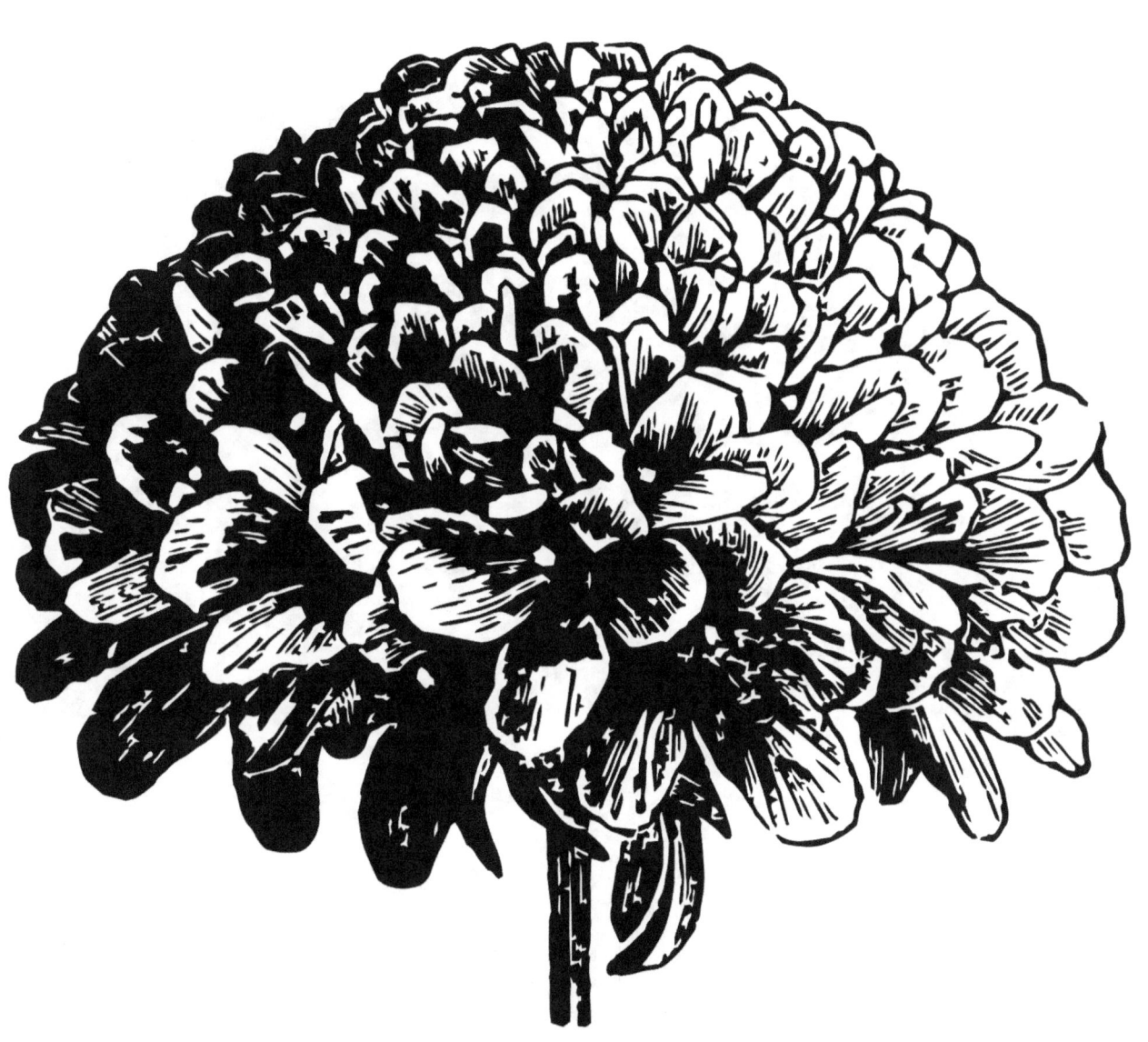

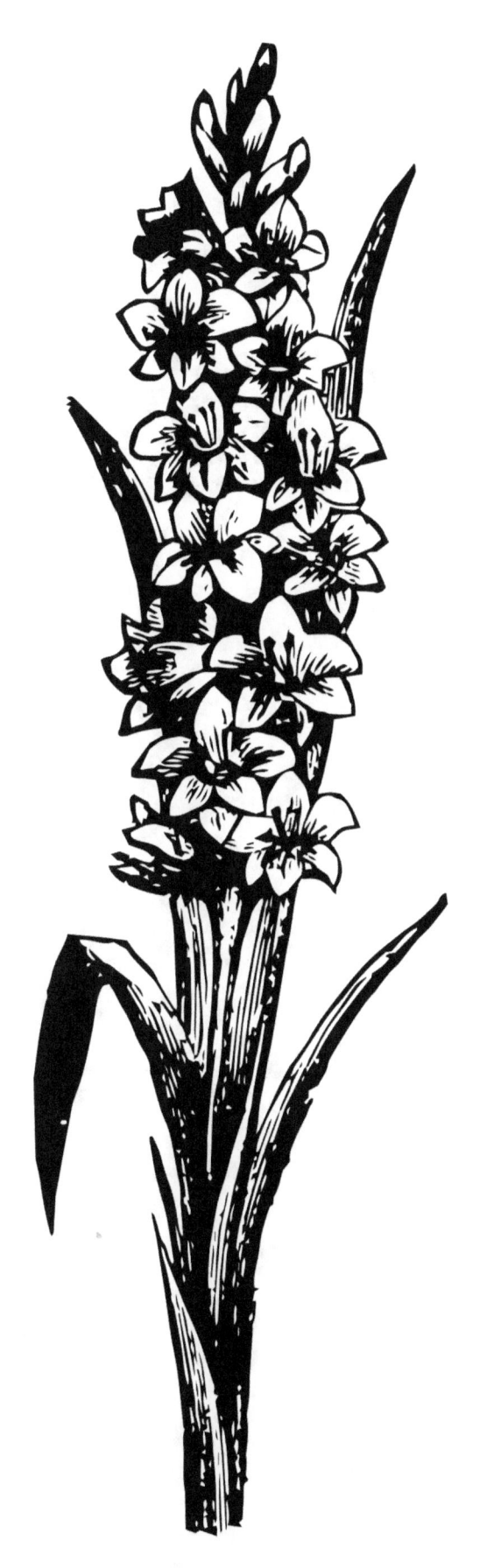

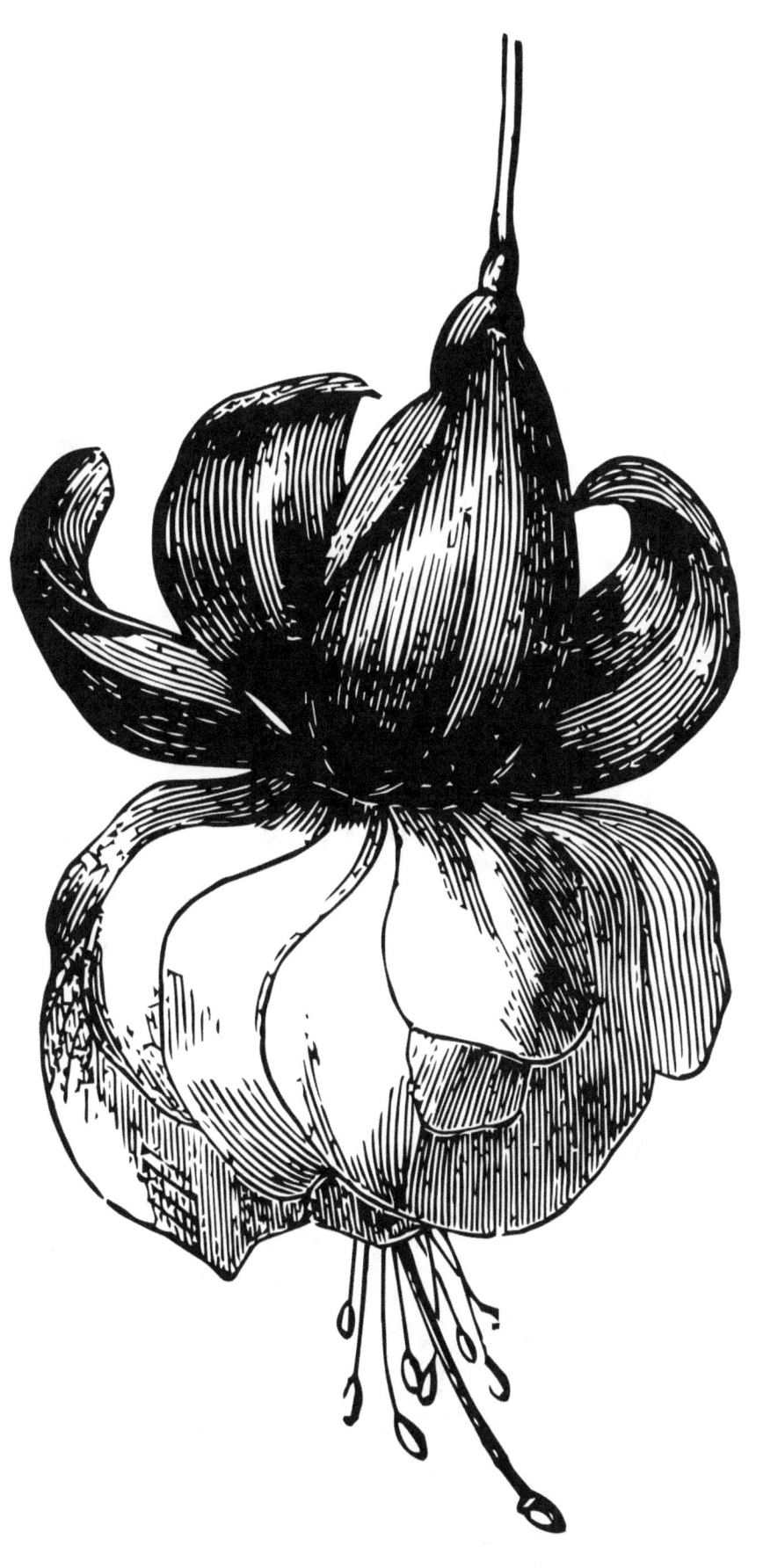

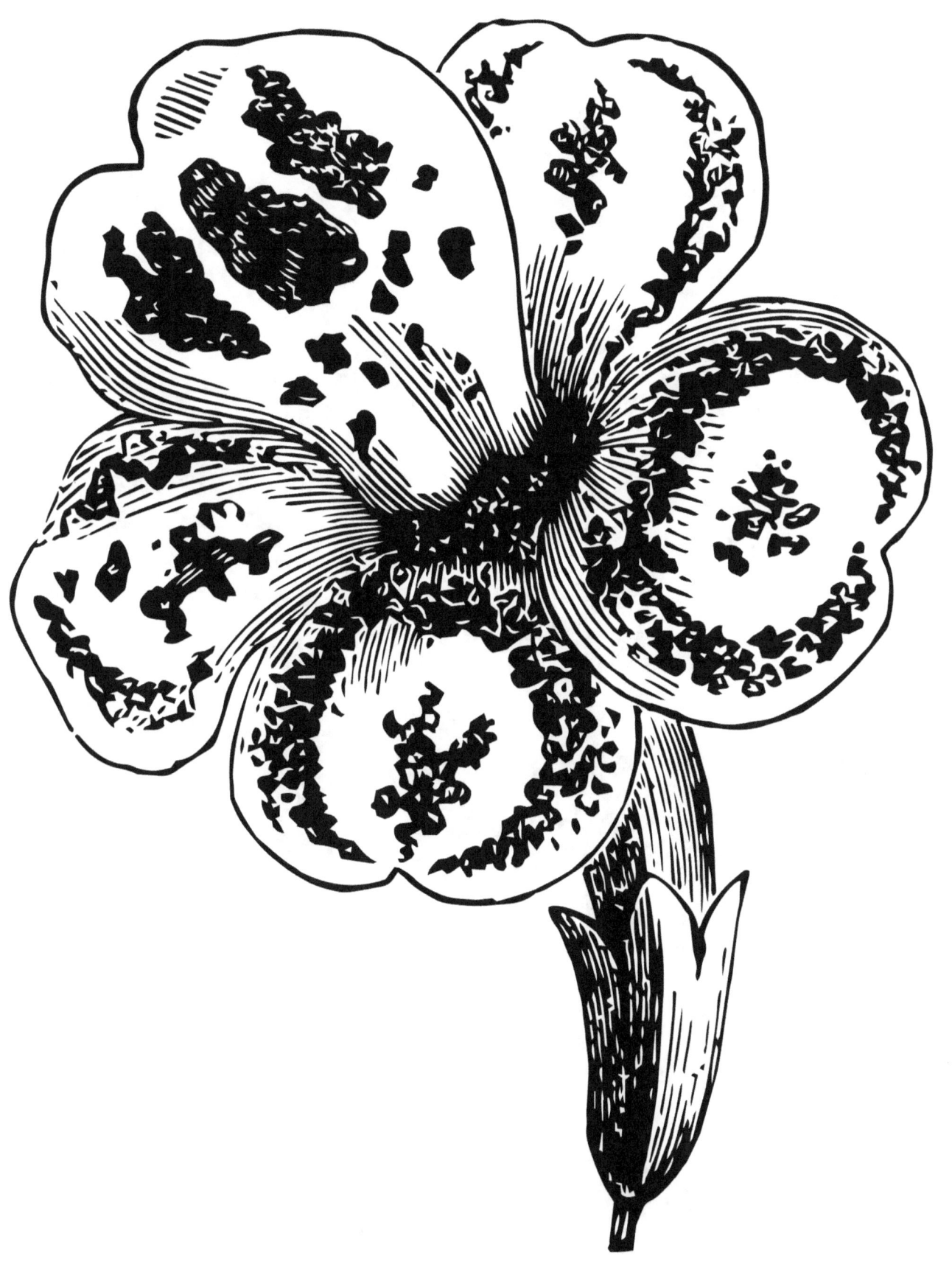

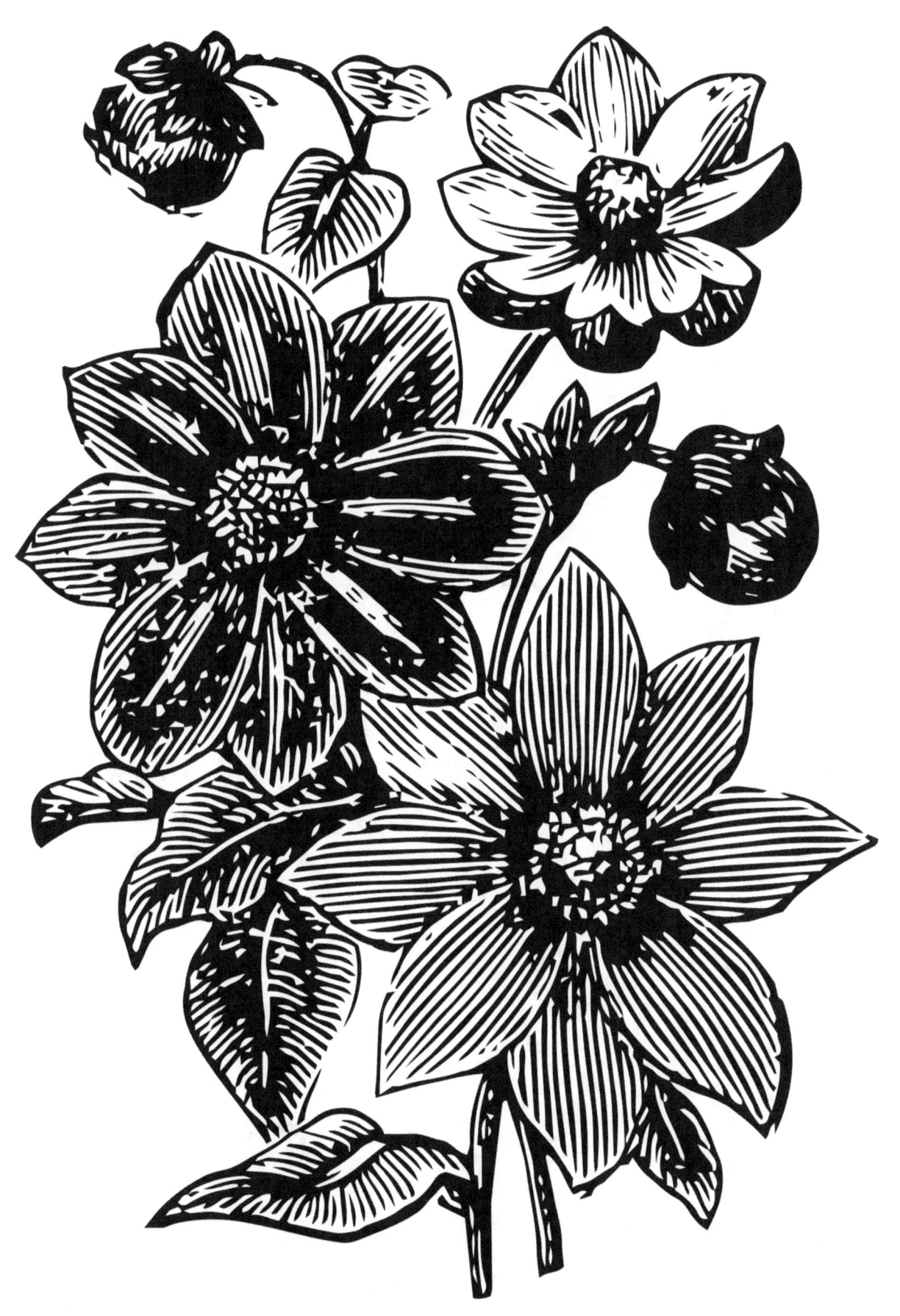

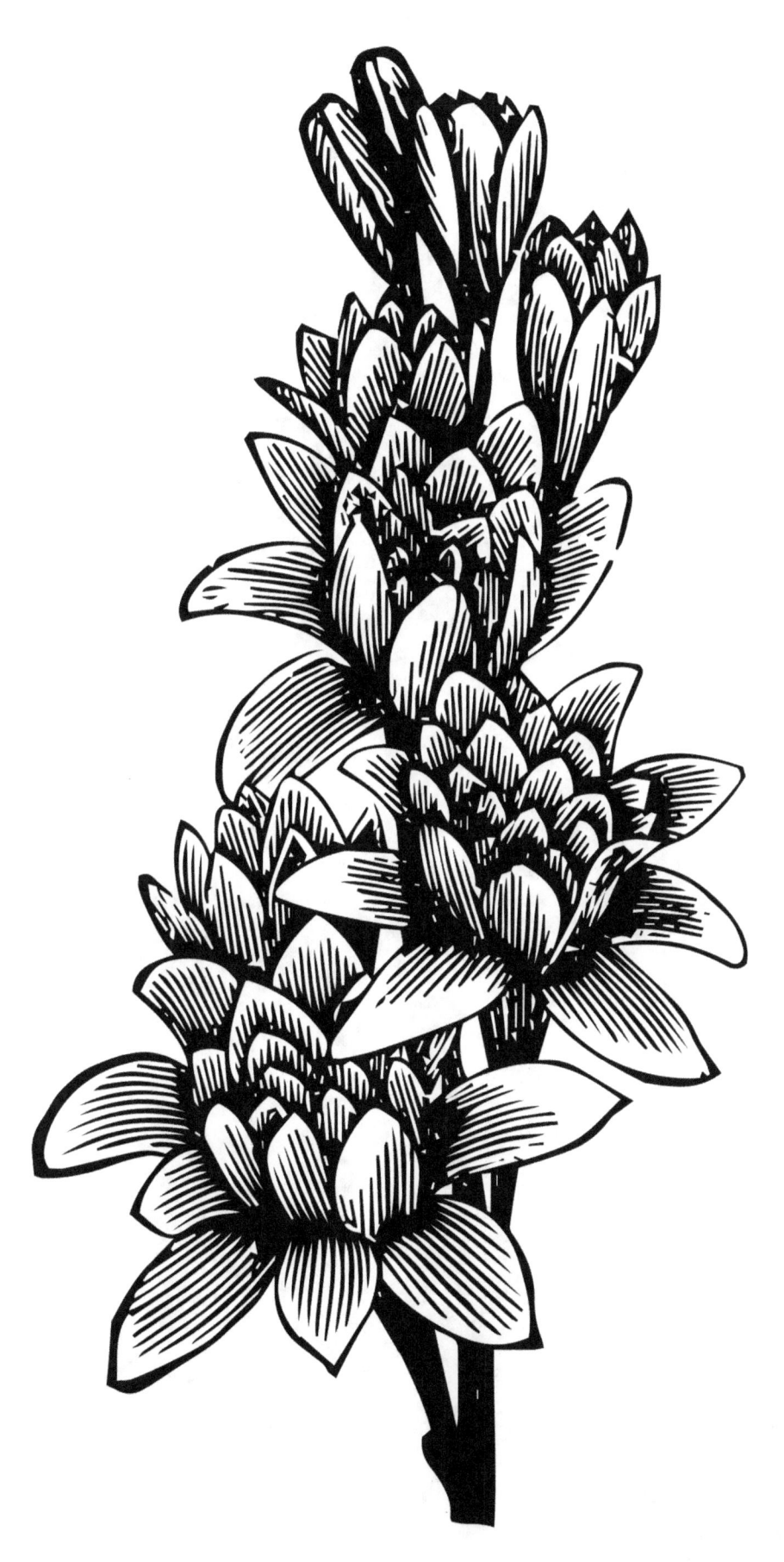

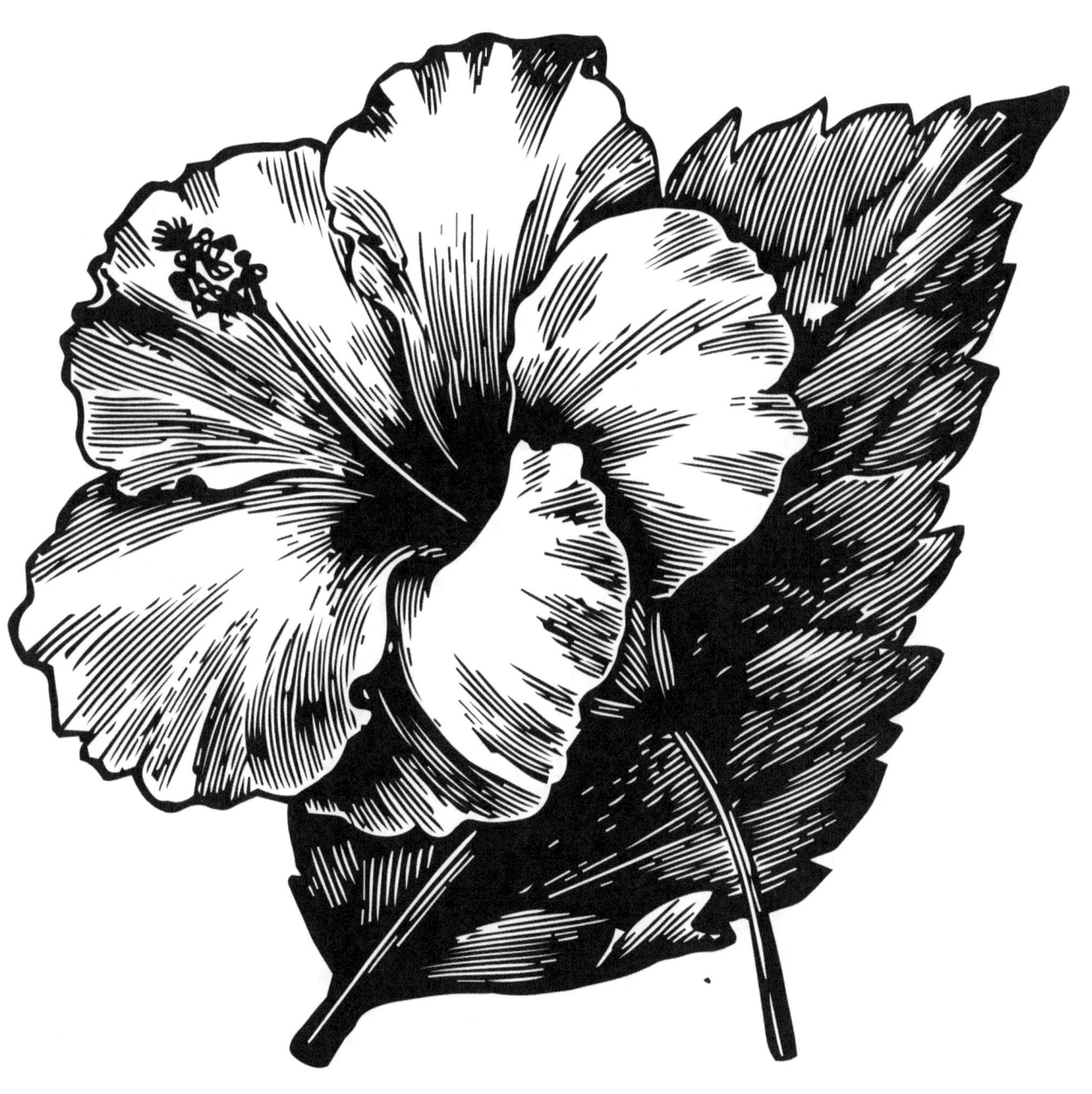

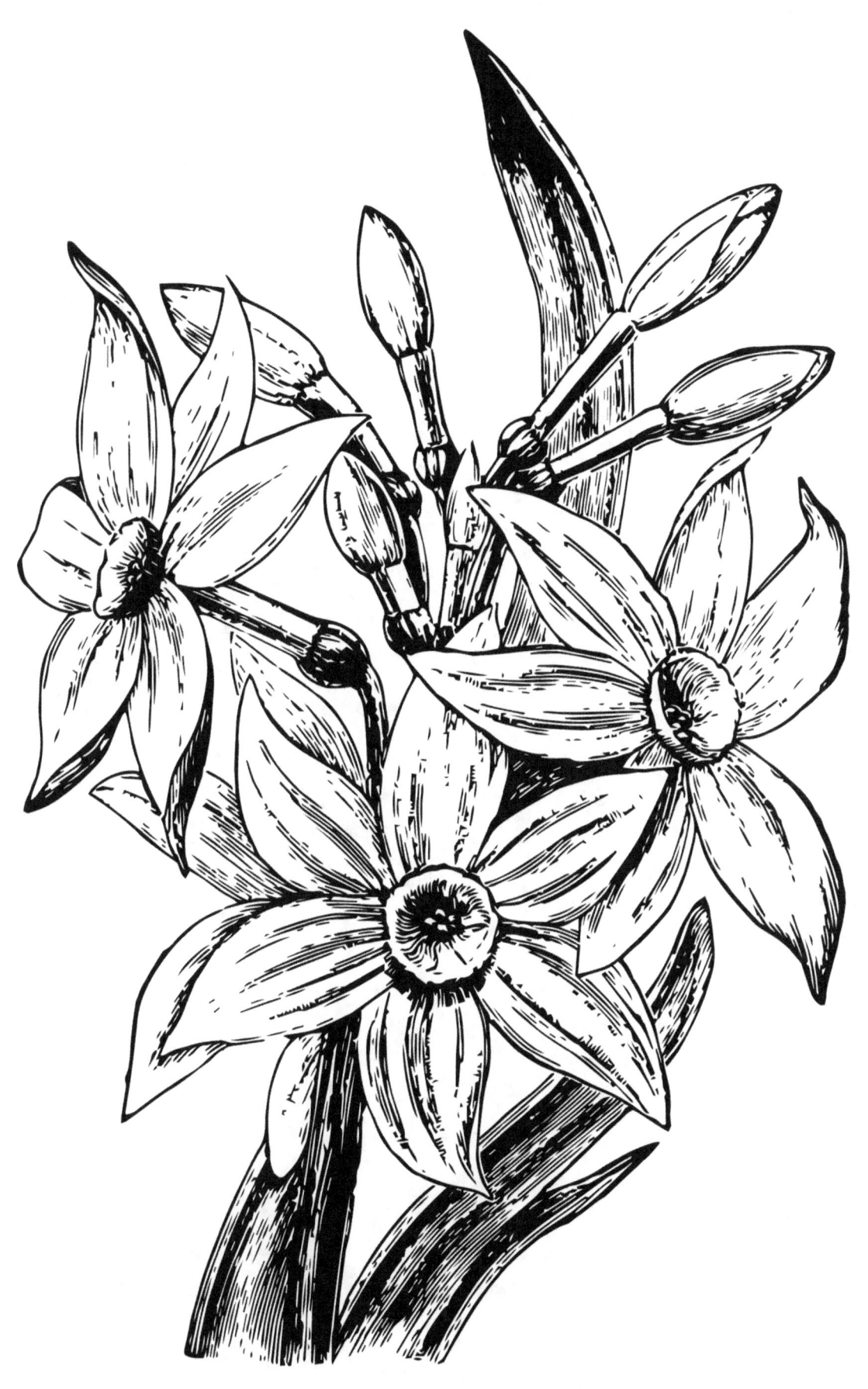

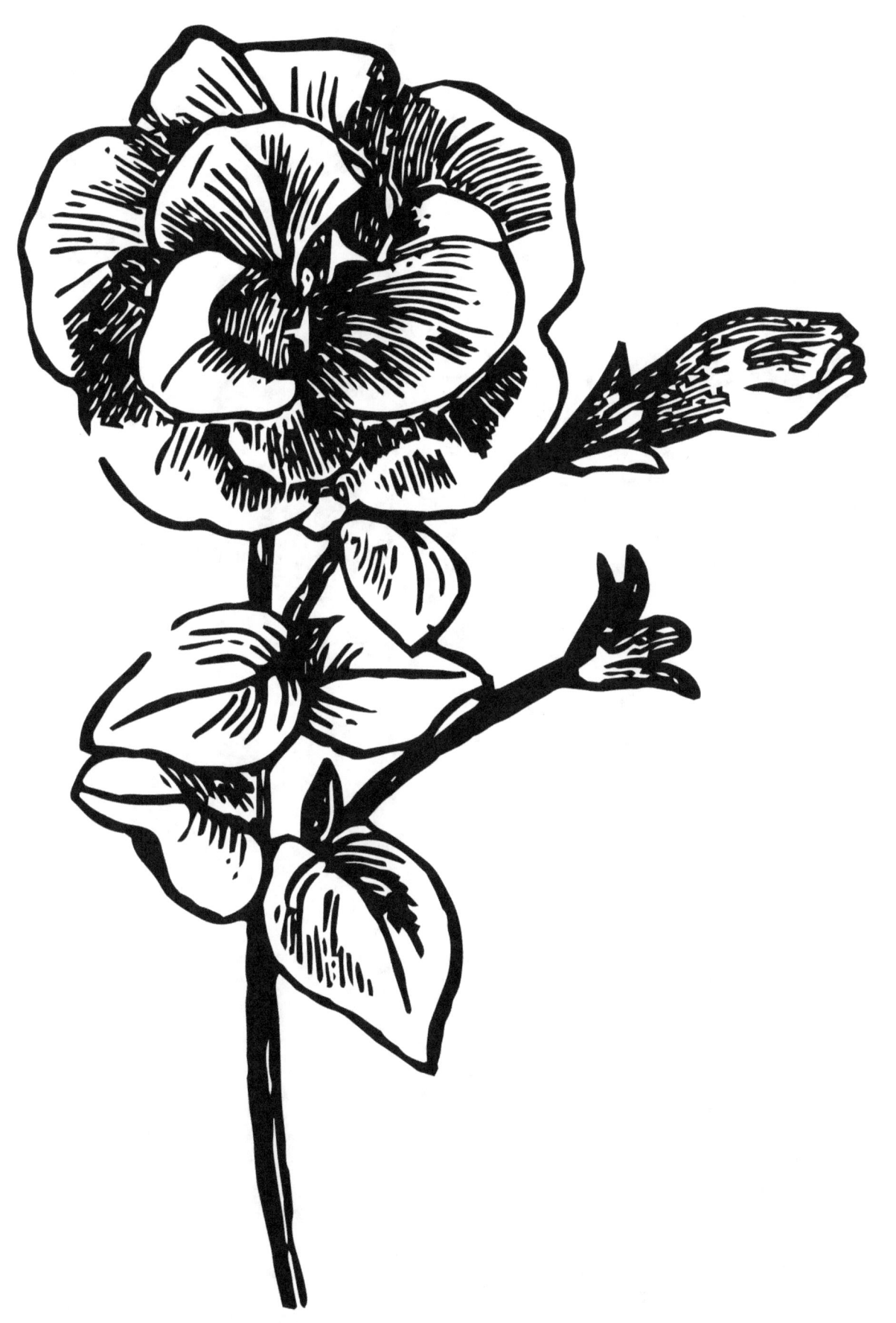

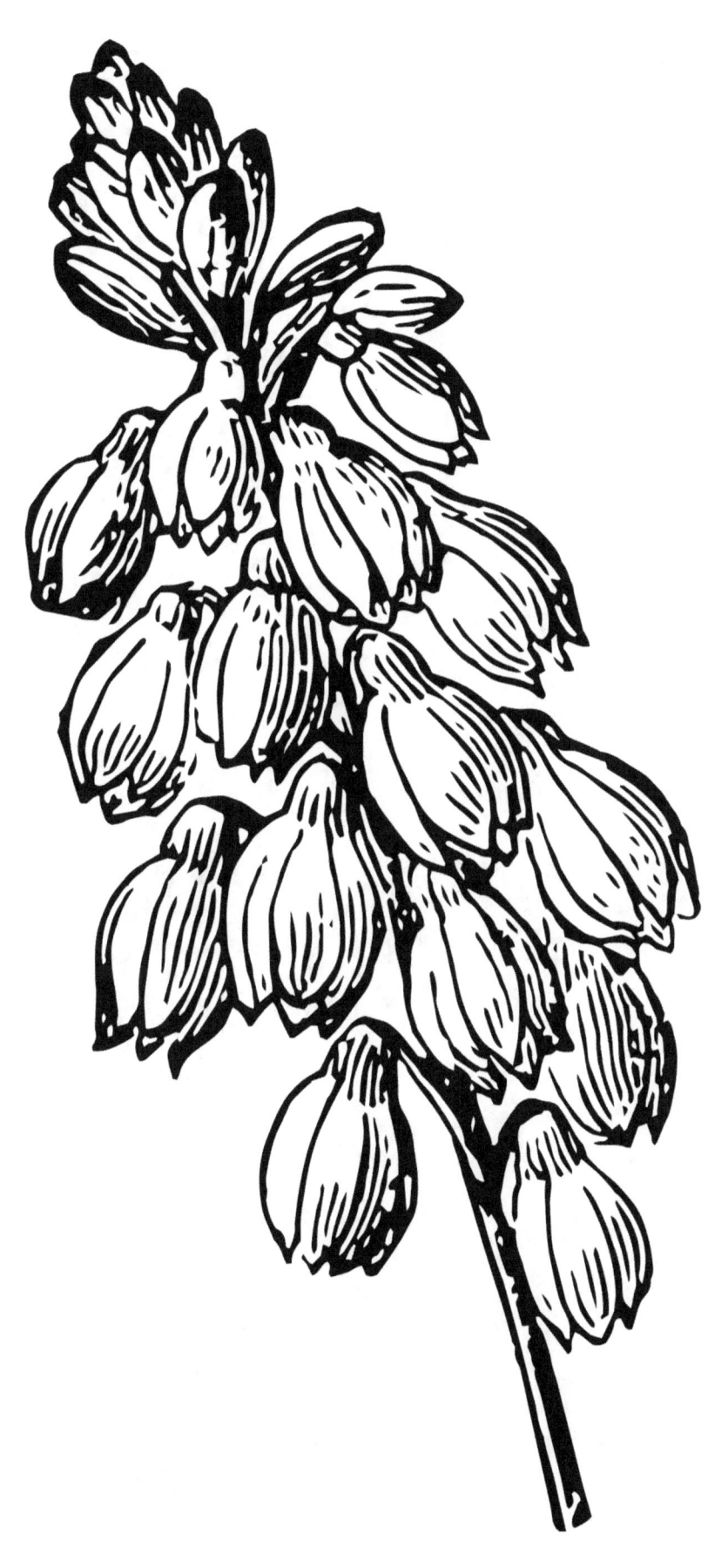

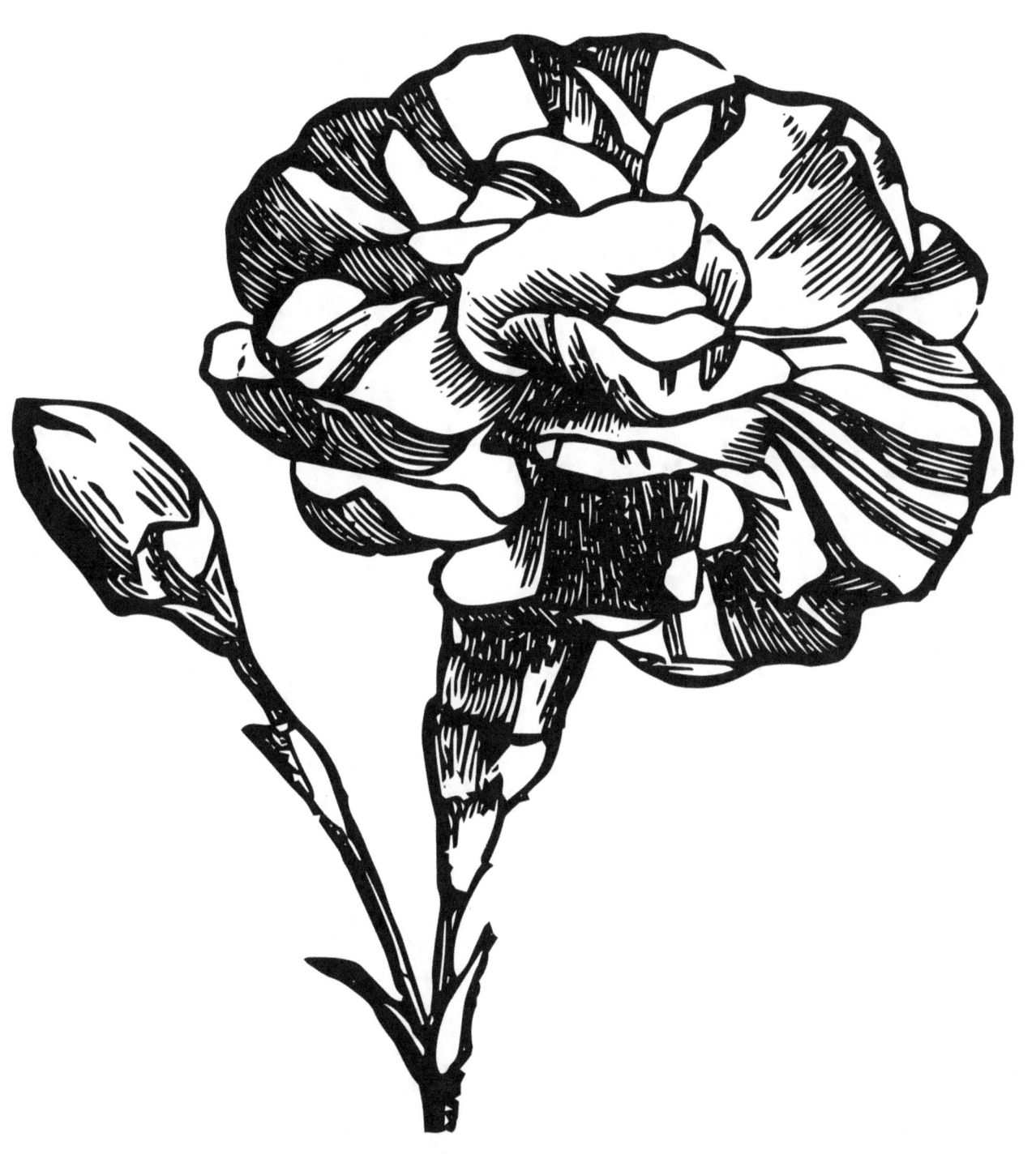

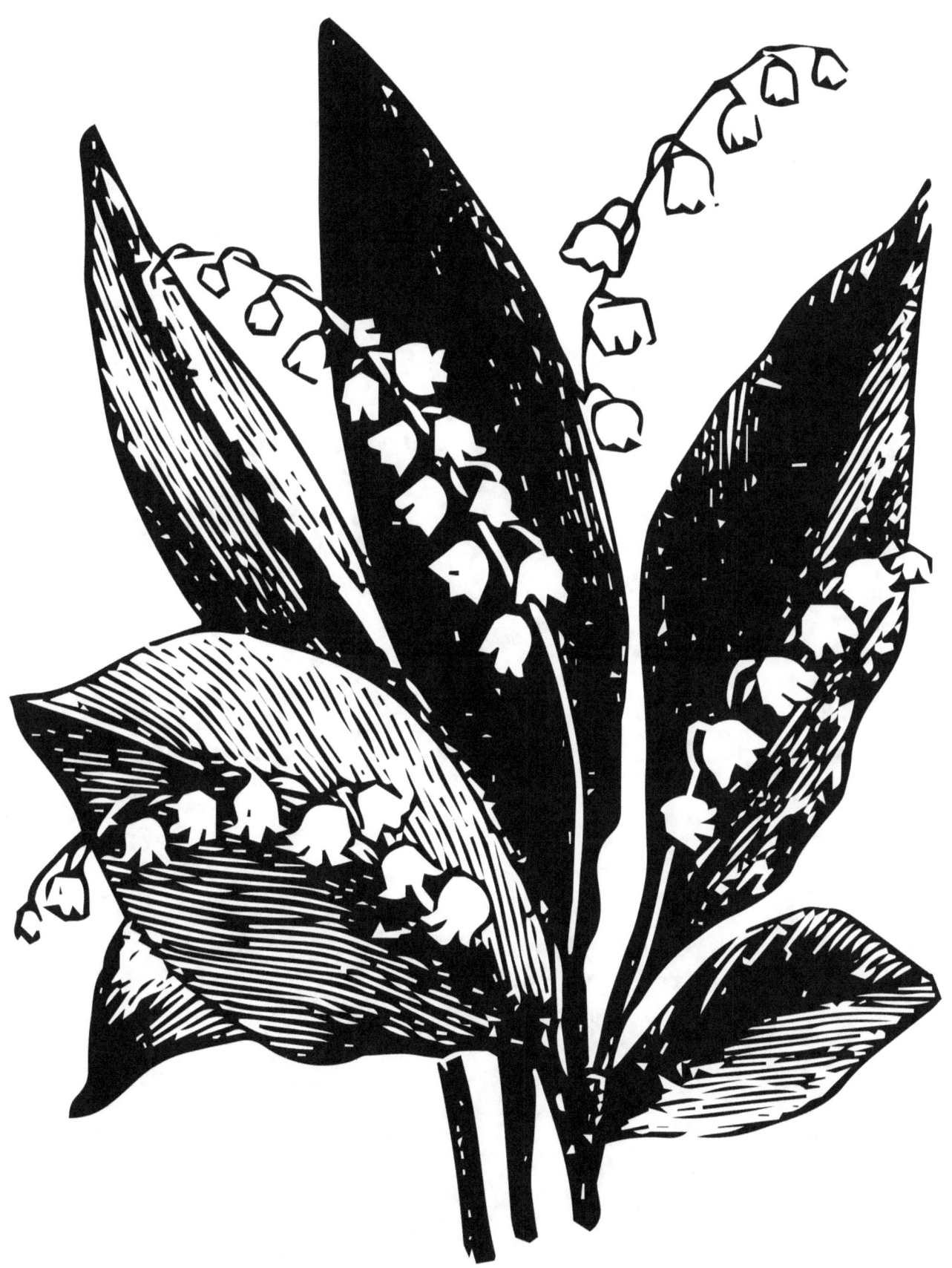

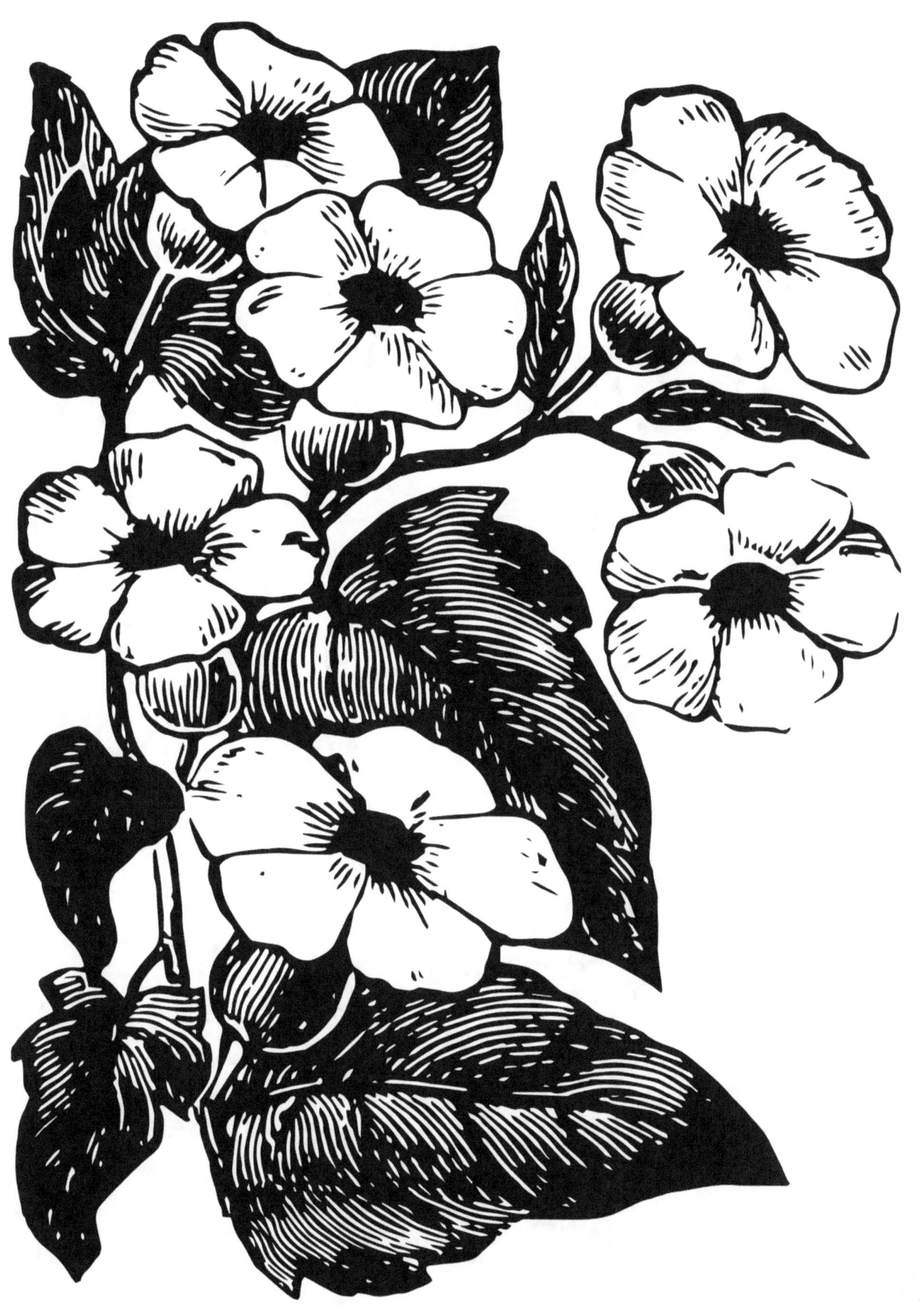

www.ingramcontent.com/pod-product-compliance
Lightning Source LLC
Chambersburg PA
CBHW081456170526
45166CB00008B/2449